# MORE FROM D.L. STEWART!

Laugh and suffer with the father of wit as he ponders:

- How he's going to pay for his college-bound daughter's refrigerator (so she won't have to eat cafeteria food), TV set (so she'll have something to do besides sitting in class), and car (so she won't have to spend *too* much time in the dormitory room he's also paying for).
- How to scare up a lunch in the house he's moving out of when his wife has moved the food, the dishes, the pots and pans to the house he's moving into.
- How he's going to make it to work in a car borrowed from his 16-year-old, a car "that's louder than Jerry Lewis and thirstier than Dean Martin."
- How to make all his dreams of being a jock come true by guiding his son into school sports . . .

"Stewart is to family men what Erma Bombeck is to family women—she the Socrates of the ironing board, he Solomon of the gray flannel suit set. . . . Stewart's wit spills over."
—*Cincinnati Enquirer*

"Until Stewart came along no one was speaking for today's American father."
—*Columbus Dispatch*

Also by D.L. Stewart

*Fathers Are People Too*

*About the Author*
D.L. Stewart is the author of the top-seller *Fathers Are People Too*. He and his wife have coauthored four children, and they all live in Beavercreek, Ohio, along with a constantly disassembling automobile, an impossible-to-assemble barbecue grill, and a Frisbee-eating dog. In addition to his books and syndicated writings, Stewart has published articles in *Good Housekeeping*, *McCalls*, and *Redbook*. He has also been a guest on such television programs as *Hour Magazine* and *The Merv Griffin Show*.

# FATHER KNOWS BEST— SOMETIMES

## D.L. STEWART

*Illustrated by Ted Pitts*

**WARNER BOOKS**

A Warner Communications Company

Warner Books, Inc., 666 Fifth Avenue, New York, NY 10103

 A Warner Communications Company

Printed in the United States of America
First Printing: June 1986
10 9 8 7 6 5 4 3 2 1


Library of Congress Cataloging-in-Publication Data

Stewart, D. L., 1942–
  Father knows best—sometimes.

  1. Fathers—Anecdotes, facetiae, satiae, etc.
I. Title.
PS3569.T4595F28  1986     813'.54      85–26562
ISBN  0-446-38194-2 (U.S.A.) (pbk.)
      0-446-38323-6 (Canada) (pbk.)

## TO ERMA,

*who showed us that it was possible to raise kids and live to tell about it.*

# CONTENTS

# FATHER KNOWS BEST — SOMETIMES

# 1

## THIS FATHER KNOWS BETTER

You lied to me, Robert Young.

But then, maybe it was my fault for being so gullible. After all, I never believed there really was a guy who rode around the Old West shooting silver bullets and punching out bad guys and spending his nights with only a white horse and an Indian. I never was dumb enough to accept a newspaperman who wore blue underwear and leaped over tall buildings and never was seen in a bar.

And yet, for some reason, I swallowed "Father Knows Best."

I actually believed there was a man who came home from work every day with a smile on his face and kissed his wife and called his kids names like "Princess" and "Bud." A man who sat around the house all evening being wise and wearing a cardigan and smoking a pipe and smiling at his family as if he had just swallowed a briefcase full of Valium.

It was not until it was too late that I realized that, not only

1

is there no such man, but father seldom knows best and usually doesn't know much of anything.

Still, I keep hoping.

I keep thinking that some day I will come home from work and the woman who promised to love, honor, and share my sitcom will be in the kitchen. She will be wearing a party frock, high heels, earrings, and a string of pearls. Her hair will be freshly coiffed. She will be holding a spoon, with which she has been stirring dinner for the last six or seven hours.

"Hi, dear," she will say. "Did you have a good day at work?"

My children will be in the living room. They will look up when I walk in. They will smile.

"Hi, Dad," they will say.

My daughter will be on the couch, wearing a sweater and a pleated skirt, with just a touch of pale lipstick on her mouth. She will be sewing. An American flag. My son will be sitting at the desk, doing his geography homework. Later, perhaps, he will come to me and ask for help. I will tell him that the capital of California is Sacramento. He will say, "Gee, thanks, Dad."

In the twenty years that I have been practicing fatherhood, it never has happened quite that way. But perhaps, I decide one day, it is my fault. If I act more like Robert Young, I reason, they will act more like the happy family that greeted him every day.

The next afternoon I am whistling as I walk into the house.

"Hi, dear," I announce, "I'm home."

The kitchen is empty. There is a note taped to the refrigerator door.

"Have taken the dog to the vet. I think she has worms. Dinner is thawing. You're out of beer."

There is no signature. But I recognize the literary style.

I walk into the living room.

My daughter is lying on the floor. She is wearing a bathrobe and a pair of striped socks, with just a touch of gold glitter on her eyelids. She is listening to rock music that is coming out of a stereo loud enough to lower her IQ.

"Hi, Princess," I shout.

"Shh," she says.

My son is at the other end of the living room. He is watching a rerun of "Gilligan's Island" with a laugh track loud enough to lower everybody's IQ.

"Hi, Bud," I shout.

"Shh," he says.

I go to the closet and look for a cardigan sweater. The only thing I can find is a sweatshirt that says, "Help Save Alligators, Eat a Preppie."

I put it on and walk back into the living room. As I get to the door I can hear my children shouting to each other.

"What's with the Bud and Princess routine?"

"Beats me. They probably had another one of those office parties today."

"Yeah. Mom'll slaughter him when she gets home."

If Robert Young lived at our house, it would take a lot more than Sanka to keep him whistling.

To be fair about it, I'm not the only one in our house who wasn't prepared for the reality of family life. The woman who promised to love, honor, and water our family tree has had some difficulties, too. Maybe it's because she never was a little boy and I never expect to be a mother, but one of the major communication gaps in our marriage concerns cleanliness.

I probably should have suspected that there was going to be a problem when I gave her the engagement ring and she boiled it for five minutes before slipping it on. Twenty years and four kids later, we have yet to reach what you would call an understanding. My definition of clean still includes any amount of dirt that is not life threatening. She continues to regard a grass stain on a pair of Levi's as the first step toward bubonic plague.

The subject seems to come up most frequently at the dinner table. In the middle of dinner one evening, for instance, she drops her fork, points at the eight-year-old and exclaims, "How can he come to the table like that?"

"Like what?" I ask, brushing a stray piece of macaroni off my lap.

"He's filthy. Look at the dirt on the back of his neck."

"How can you see the back of his neck? He's sitting across the table from you."

"It's my job to see things like that."

"So, what if it is dirty? He doesn't eat with his neck. What's the difference?"

"I'll tell you what the difference is. The difference is that it looks terrible. I work all day to keep this house clean and then they come home from school and turn it into the La Brea Tar Pits. I don't know where they get it."

"Beats me," I say, transferring a smear of catsup from my sleeve to the tablecloth. "But I really think you're making a big deal out of nothing. Kids are supposed to get dirty. I think it's in the Constitution somewhere. Anyway, he's only eight years old. He'll outgrow it."

"Oh yeah? What about the sixteen-year-old? I'll bet it's been two years since he's washed behind his ears."

"With all that hair, I'll bet it's been two years since anybody's seen his ears. My guess is that he left them in his locker in ninth grade and he's been listening through his nose ever since then."

The sixteen-year-old ignores us and continues eating. Either that, or he can't hear us. After dinner she sends the kids off to the bathtub, burns their clothes, and joins me in the living room for a cup of tea.

"I really think you're making too big a deal out of this cleanliness thing," I point out. "You just have to remember that boys are a little messier than girls. I can remember walking to school one day and coming across this big pile of dirt at a construction site. I must have played in that thing for two hours. By the time I got to school, my clothes were filthy and my books were a mess."

"Your teachers were probably pretty mad about that, I'll bet."

"Not really. It was a very liberal college. The point is, a little bit of dirt never hurt anybody."

"So you think I'm too fussy?"

"Well, I wouldn't say that. But I did notice that you seem to be the only mother in the neighborhood who makes her kids take off their shoes when they come home from school."

"What do you mean? I know lots of mothers who make their kids take off their shoes."

"Sure, before they come into the house. Not before they come into the yard."

"You'd do that, too, if you'd just spent six hours cleaning and then watched them roll through your living room like the Johnstown flood. Those aren't kids, they're mud slides with freckles."

"Well, don't get discouraged. Eventually they'll grow out of that stage. I promise."

"I hope so," she sighs. She gets up and goes outside to vacuum the backyard. I get up and wipe up the tea that I have spilled on the couch.

I suspect that we never will reach total agreement about how kids should act.

She doesn't understand how a kid can get dirty sitting on the couch, talking on the telephone, doing his homework, or walking from the bathtub to his bedroom.

I tend to be suspicious of any boy who isn't packing at least a pound of dirt on his body at all times.

She wants to know why a sixteen-year-old can't drink milk without spilling it, an eleven-year-old can't look at milk without spilling it, and an eight-year-old eats soup with his fingers.

I have a dozen shirts with spaghetti stains on the fronts.

She worries when she sees our kids climbing a tree, jumping down a flight of stairs, or leaning out of a second-story window.

I figure a leap or two off the top of a garage is the only way a kid will ever be able to find out for sure whether he can fly.

When the sixteen-year-old broke his hand playing football, she was afraid it would affect his handwriting and his schoolwork.

I wondered if it would have any permanent effect on his down-and-out passes.

When any of them cough, sneeze twice in a row, complain about a headache, or hint that they don't feel well, she rushes to Dr. Spock.

I tell them to go outside and play.

She asks me how our youngest can be so gross sometimes.

I don't think it's that unusual for an eight-year-old boy to want to find out if it's possible to shoot a dead caterpillar out of his cap gun.

It really seems to bother her that three boys can't ride in the backseat of a car together for more than five minutes without getting into a fight.

I think there's something wrong with a kid who doesn't punch his brother every half hour or so.

She thinks two tacos should be enough to feed a sixteen-year-old boy.

I think two tacos is something a sixteen-year-old boy eats while he's waiting for his six burritos.

She wonders out loud why the eight-year-old is forever taking off his glasses and forgetting where he left them.

I've been looking for my watch for the last four days.

She gets a little irritated when our daughter finds out that she has a soccer game in three weeks but never tells anybody about it until thirty minutes before she wants us to drive her there.

I keep meaning to mention the dinner we're supposed to go to tonight.

She gets really irritated when pillows get thrown, lamps get knocked over, knickknacks get broken, and house plants wind up standing in a pile of broken limbs.

I think the living room is a great place for a football game on a cold winter night when television is lousy and there's nothing else to do.

She is constantly reminding the kids to brush their teeth and comb their hair before they go to bed.

I keep wondering who's going to see them in bed.

Sometimes I think she really wasn't cut out to raise kids.

But whenever I suggest that to her, she always points out that she's raising one more than I am.

# 2

## IT'S A LONG WAY FROM SPRINGFIELD, U.S.A.

Robert Young and his annoyingly wonderful television family lived in Springfield, U.S.A. He was an insurance man who owned the world's largest collection of cardigan sweaters. He and his wife, Margaret, had three beautiful children, none of whom ever smoked, drank, lied, swore, or had a pimple.

My family lives in Beavercreek, Ohio. I am a newspaperman with the largest collection of Nehru jackets this side of New Delhi. The woman who promised to love, honor, and fertilize my family tree and I have four children, each of whom calls the ACLU every time we ask them to make their beds.

But I guess what bothers me most about the Anderson family was that the problems Jim Anderson solved each week were not real problems. They always were things like: Should Princess go out on a date with the Phi Beta Kappa from Harvard or stay home and help her mother bake brownies? Should Bud accept the Fullbright Fellowship before he finishes junior high? Is twelve too young for Kitten to start going to the bathroom by herself?

Never, for instance, did we see Princess come home from a date at three in the morning. On the handlebars of a Harley-Davidson. Just once I would like to have seen how wise Jim Anderson would have been if Bud had walked into the house wearing an earring.

Not only did they not seem to ever have any realistic major problems, they never even ran into the ordinary hassles that regular families encounter. Like, finding a babysitter.

Actually, when we had only one child, it was easy to find babysitters. All we had to do was let it be known that we had a cuddly infant to watch for the evening, and our place would be overrun with sweet, gray-haired grandmothers.

When our second kid came along, it got a little tougher to find someone to sit with them, and most of the gray-haired grandmothers came armed with long knitting needles.

By the time our brood grew to three, it was almost impossible to find anyone to stay alone with them for more than half an hour, and the few old ladies who showed up had tattoos on their shoulders and .45s in their pocketbooks.

Now that our herd numbers four, the only ones who will take a chance with them have faces that I recognize from post office walls.

All of which does not make me overly optimistic when we start looking for someone to stay with them while we're on our winter getaway vacation in Florida.

The getaway vacation to Florida, incidentally, is not my idea. It's just something that evolved as a result of a marriage-full of Ohio winters.

Every year it would be the same depressing story. Sometime in the middle of January, the mercury would fall like a bad stock, the kids would spend all day in the house because it was too cold to go outside, and when I came home from work the woman who promised to love, honor, and raise my temperature would be barricaded in the bedroom.

The first time it happens I call a friend who has been married most of his life.

"Sounds like cabin fever," he says. "Get her out of the house, quick."

"OK," I agree. "We'll take the kids and go to a movie tonight."

"Are you dense? Taking the kids is not what she needs. I mean, if she was hooked on gambling, would you take her for a weekend in Las Vegas? You've got to take her out alone."

"Yeah, but that's going to cost money. I'll have to find a babysitter, then there's the cost of movie tickets. And gas. And Milk Duds."

"Suit yourself, Diamond Jim. Winter will be over in another couple of months. I'm sure she'll open the bedroom door as soon as it's spring."

We catch the early show that evening. She laughs hysterically all the way through it. I, on the other hand, didn't think *Psycho* was all that funny.

The same thing happens the following winter.

"OK, c'mon out," I shout through the bedroom door. "We'll go to a movie."

"That's not going to do it," she shouts back. "One crummy box of popcorn with extra butter is not going to cure my problem."

"You're being melodramatic. It can't be all that bad."

"How would you know? You spend your whole day hanging around with adults. You have no concept of what it's like to be cooped up all day with a bunch of kids who make enough noise to give Helen Keller a migraine. So far today I have tied forty-three tennis shoes, wiped seven pounds of peanut butter off of cupboard doors, and seen enough bloody noses to nauseate Dracula. Do you know what the high spot of my afternoon has been?"

"No, what?"

"Preventing the six-year-old from climbing up inside the chimney to see if Santa had forgotten any toys."

"You sound testy."

"Jack the Ripper was testy. I'm going out of my mind."

That night we go to a movie and dinner.

With each succeeding year, the price of unlocking that door gets a little steeper. From dinner and a movie, we progress to dinner, a movie, and dancing. Then to a night out at a local hotel. A night at a hotel in a nearby town. A weekend in a hotel at a neighboring town.

So on the day I come home and see a sign on our door that says, "This area protected by vicious guard dogs," I know it's going to cost me a few bucks.

"Open up," I call, "it's me."

"How do I know it's you and not one of those sneaky kids disguising his voice?" she calls back. "Say something in adult."

"Don't be ridiculous. It's me and you're having your annual attack of cabin fever, and the sooner you open the door the sooner we can decide what to do about it."

She slides the triple dresser away from the door and lets me in.

"So, what'll it be this year? Dinner and a show? A weekend on the town?"

"I don't know. I just want to go somewhere where there are no kids and it's warm enough so that we'll see people who aren't all bundled up in clothes."

"How about a weekend at a burlesque house?"

"I was thinking more along the lines of Florida."

"You're kidding. Do you have any idea of what it costs to spend a weekend in Florida at this time of year?"

"I happen to know that you have some money put away."

"That's the money I'm saving for a down payment on a new car."

"Fine. Just go ahead and buy your new car. You can use it to drive up to see me on visiting days at the farm."

"Well, all right, we'll go to Florida for the weekend. But we may have trouble finding a babysitter. Let's face it, the list of people who would want to stay with this bunch for a weekend has dwindled considerably since the Marquis de Sade died."

"You're exaggerating," she says. "I'm sure we won't have

any trouble finding someone to stay with them. They're lovely, sweet children."

"So how come we're spending our life savings to ditch these sweet, lovely children?"

"Because they're driving me right up the wall. Now help me think of someone who could handle them."

"I don't think the Pittsburgh Steelers are doing anything this weekend."

"Be serious. If we don't find somebody in the next few days, we're going to have to skip the trip."

"OK. How about relatives?"

"I've already tried them. Do you think it means anything that my mother's phone, your mother's phone, and my Aunt Vi's phone all are out of order?"

"Probably just an amazing coincidence. Have you tried all of our close friends?"

"People with four kids to babysit have no close friends."

Two nights before we are scheduled to leave, she still is phoning around for a babysitter. Finally, in the middle of one call, she puts her hand over the mouthpiece and signals excitedly to me.

"I think I've found one," she whispers. "She's twenty-one years old and she's had a lot of experience with children. What other things do we need to know about her?"

"Ask her if she can bring her own whip and chair."

"No, I mean do you think I should ask her some questions about herself? You know, should I sort of screen her?"

"Did Hirohito screen his kamikaze pilots? Just tell her what time to show up and hope she doesn't catch on until our plane is in the air."

The next day the babysitter comes over to meet with us and review some of the things she'll need to know. We explain the kids' schedules to her and show her how to find the three days' worth of frozen pizza that they'll probably polish off before we get to the airport. We hand her a list of phone numbers she might need: pediatrician, ambulance, fire department, SWAT team.

After she is gone, I mention to the woman who promised to love, honor, and turn on my siren that the babysitter appears to be very level-headed and capable.

"I'm sure she is," she agrees, hesitantly. "But, somehow it seems sort of strange, leaving the kids with somebody that young. The ones we had before have always had gray hair."

"Don't worry," I assure her. "By the time we get back, so will this one."

Even though finding a babysitter is a real chore, I have to admit that the trip to Florida has some appeal to me, too. If nothing else, I'll have a chance to sleep in on Saturday morning.

Ever since they were old enough to knot their sheets into ropes and climb over the sides of their cribs, our kids have been warned never to wake us on Saturday mornings.

There are exceptions, of course. If the house is on fire, they are permitted to use the phone in our room to call the fire department. And they may wake us if they are sick, but only if they have a note from the Mayo Clinic and two sets of X-rays.

The rules are clear. The policy is firm. And the last time no one woke us on a Saturday morning was in October of 1973. That was the morning they fed pancakes to the dog and she got sick and they cleaned it up. With my tennis shorts.

But the Saturday morning a few weeks ago is more typical.

The first kid comes into our bedroom at 7:30. It is the eight-year-old. He is crying softly. I open one eye.

"This better be important," I snarl. It is not that I am insensitive, but I learned a long time ago that a kid who is crying softly never is hurt and probably only wants to fink on his brother.

He goes to his mother's side of the bed. He whispers something to her. She mumbles something to him. He leaves.

"What was that?" I ask.

"The eleven-year-old ate all the Froot Loops. I told him to make peanut butter toast instead."

I go back to sleep. Forty winks later the eight-year-old is back. He is crying. He whispers to his mother. She mumbles back. He leaves.

"What was it this time?"

"The eleven-year-old ate all the peanut butter. I told him to make oatmeal."

Twenty winks later he returns. Crying. Whispers. Mumbles. He leaves.

"Don't tell me. The eleven-year-old ate all the oatmeal and drank all the milk."

"He ate all the sugar."

Ten winks later there is a scratching noise on the door. It is the dog. It can mean only one of two things. Either she wants to go out or the eleven-year-old ate all the Alpo. I get up and let her out. I crawl back into bed.

A wink and a half later the eleven-year-old comes in. He is crying. Probably from stomach cramps.

He whispers to his mother. She mumbles back. He leaves.

"Now what?" I ask.

"They're having an argument over the television."

"He planning on eating that, too?"

"No. He wants to watch cartoons and the sixteen-year-old is watching MTV."

Eight Duran Duran's, three Men at Work, and a Def Leppard later, the bedroom wall begins to shake. Either the San Andreas fault has moved east or the sixteen-year-old is knocking on the door.

"What is it?" I shout.

"Ask Mom where my basketball socks are."

I ask. They are in his dresser.

"In your dresser."

Two minutes later the room trembles again.

"What?" I shout.

"Where's my dresser?"

I ask. It is under his overdue library books.

Five entire minutes go by before the door opens again. It is the eleven-year-old.

"Phone for you," he says.

"Find out who it is and what they want," I say, pulling the covers up over my head.

A minute later he returns.

"It's some lady from Planned Parenthood," he says.

"Don't let her hang up. I'll be right there."

As it turns out, I never do get to sleep in on Saturday morning because, the day before we are to leave for our getaway weekend in Florida, the babysitter calls. When she hangs up, the woman who promised to love, honor, and break it to me gently begins to sob hysterically and bash the phone against the refrigerator.

"Bad news?" I inquire.

"That was the babysitter," she moans. "She can't make it."

"Did she say why?"

"I don't know. She just made some feeble excuse about her life insurance being cancelled and hung up."

"Well, it looks like we'll have to forget the trip."

"Not so fast," she says. "I've been doing a little figuring. Do you have any idea how long it's been since I've been by myself for more than twenty-four hours at a time?"

"No. But I'll bet with the right kind of coaxing I can get you to tell me."

"It's been twenty years, one husband, four kids, three cats, a dog, and 12,000 car pools. How can they call this the land of the free when when there are women in it who have never spent more than two consecutive days without hearing the sound of a knock on the bathroom door?"

"Well, I sympathize with your problem. But, if we don't have a babysitter, what can we do about it?"

"I'll just go alone. My old college roommate lives in Miami and I can spend some time visiting with her. Or I can wade in the ocean or sit around the pool or go shopping or whatever I feel like. Anything just to have some time to myself and not have to worry about whose turn it is to drive to soccer practice."

So on Friday afternoon I drive her to the airport, kiss her and our American Express card goodbye, and drive home. As I am pulling into the driveway, I hear the phone ringing. I rush inside and answer it. It is the woman who promised to love, honor, and reach out and touch somebody.

"Don't tell me you're in Miami already?" I ask.

"Of course not. The plane was delayed and I'm still at the airport. I just wanted to remind you to be sure that the eight-year-old takes his yellow medicine. It's on the kitchen counter."

"Don't worry. I'll remember. Have a good time in Miami."

I hang up and fix dinner. An hour and a half later we are at the table. The phone rings. I answer it.

"Hello?"

"It's me. I'm in Atlanta waiting for my connection. Have you eaten dinner yet?"

"We're right in the middle of it."

"Good. Tell the eleven-year-old he has to have at least one helping of green beans. And yell at the sixteen-year-old to quit leaning back in his chair. He's going to break it."

I tell her not to worry, hang up, and return to the dining room. The eleven-year-old is slipping his green beans to the dog. The sixteen-year-old is teetering his chair back on its hind legs. I am impressed. The Amazing Kreskin would be impressed.

Two hours later the phone rings. I answer it.

"How's the weather in Miami?" I ask.

"How did you know it was me?" she asks.

"Lucky guess. What is it this time?"

"Are the kids in bed?"

"I just sent the two little ones upstairs a few minutes ago."

"Well, get the eight-year-old back up and have him brush his teeth."

"What makes you think he hasn't already done it? I reminded him just before he went upstairs."

"That doesn't mean a thing. He could be standing in front of the bathroom sink when you remind him and he'd still forget. I've seen him go to bed with a dry toothbrush in his hand."

"All right. I'll get him up again. Anything else?"

"Let the dog in."

"Check."

She spends three days in Miami. We get a long-distance call from her every other hour on the hour. Between the phone bill, the airfare, and the hotel bill, it turns out to be a pretty expensive trip.

But then, I suppose it was worth it, as long as it helped her get her mind off of her family for a while.

# 3

## THE GRADUATE

She walked to the stage tall and proud in her white gown, and they announced her name and handed her a diploma and a single red rose.

And in that moment the world saw one more young woman graduating. But from our seats, high up in the auditorium, we didn't see that at all.

We saw an infant, pink and angry, newly taken from her mother's body, using the first few breaths of her life to complain about the indignity of it all.

The world saw a young woman who carried herself with grace and beauty as she moved.

But we saw a baby grown fat and healthy on her mother's milk and Gerber's strained apricots taking her first top-heavy steps across the living room floor, lunging the final few inches into her father's arms.

The world saw a young woman who can't wait to move into a place of her own, free of her parents, free of the rules and the limits and the curfews they place on her.

We saw a little girl who cried when the babysitter arrived.

The world saw a young woman of calm assurance, eager to experience whatever it is that life has in store for her.

We saw a little girl with long, straight hair and skinned-up knees standing at the front door tearfully looking out, waiting for the bus to come and take her away to her first full day of school.

The world saw a young woman who thinks clearly and reasons well and speaks with confidence.

We saw a little girl who confused her *A* sounds with her *B* sounds and told everybody that her grandmother lived in a bepartment in Cleveland.

The world saw a young woman filled with poise.

We saw a junior-high girl making her first appearance in a gymnastics meet on legs that trembled so much she barely made it across the balance beam.

The world saw a young woman eager for travel, impatient to return to the places she has enjoyed, ready to go to the places she has never seen.

We saw an adolescent who turned our family vacation trip to Chicago into a series of hasty stops and frantic window openings and long clean-up delays.

The world saw a young woman who was strong and proud and independent.

We saw a teenager who wanted a prom dress and knew just how to look at her father with big brown eyes until he paid for it.

The world saw a young woman of good taste.

We saw a teenager who painted black stripes across her bedroom walls.

The world saw a young woman who is calm and logical and prepared to take on almost anything.

We saw a new driver who stalled trying to get a stick-shift car through a busy downtown intersection. Six consecutive times.

The world saw her the way she is.

We tend to see her the way she used to be.

And maybe that will never change. Maybe we never will see her the way the world does. But the world can never love her the way we do.

Not that it always was easy. I mean, I knew that having a daughter was going to mean long waits to use the phone and even longer waits to use the bathroom. But how could I have anticipated that, when she was fifteen, we would be confronted with the "great prom crisis."

It starts out smoothly enough. Everything is all arranged. The fifteen-year-old is going to go to the prom with her boyfriend, Bruce. They are going to double-date with their friends, Eddie and Karen. Eddie is going to drive his car. I am going to stay up all night and think nasty thoughts about teenage boys.

Three days before the prom, Eddie and Karen break up. Everything is all unarranged. The fifteen-year-old and her boyfriend don't have a ride. Karen doesn't have a date. I'm still going to have to stay up all night, because I'm going to have to pick them up when the after-prom is over.

"Too bad life isn't like the old 'Father Knows Best' show," I say to the fifteen-year-old.

"Why?"

"Well, if this happened, Jim Anderson would have gone upstairs to the attic and dug out his old tuxedo and taken the girl to the prom. And everybody would have had a great time and stood around smiling and saying what a great guy ol' Jim was."

"That's a neat idea," the fifteen-year-old says. "Let's do that."

"Don't be ridiculous. I don't even know Jim Anderson. Besides, I don't think he'd come all this way to go to a prom."

"Not Jim. You."

"Me?"

"Sure. You've got a tuxedo. You could take Karen and we could double-date."

"That's silly. Why would Karen want to go to the prom with me? I'm old enough to be her, uh, big brother."

"But if she says yes, will you do it?"

"Well, sure, I guess so," I agree. I am not too worried. Karen is only sixteen. She certainly is not going to want to be seen at the prom with a thirty-seven-year-old man. No matter how devilishly handsome he is.

The next day the fifteen-year-old comes home from school and tells me Karen has accepted my invitation.

Suddenly I am faced with a whole bunch of questions seldom answered by Ann Landers. What's going to happen when people find out I'm taking Karen to the prom? Will Eddie get jealous and beat me up? Will Karen's father beat me up? How much are the alimony payments going to be? It's not easy, being a thirty-seven-year-old teenager.

On the day before the prom the fifteen-year-old calls me at work.

"Don't forget to pick up the corsage on your way home," she says.

"Corsage?"

"The corsage you ordered for Karen. You did remember to order her a corsage, didn't you?"

"Of course I did. I'm not senile, you know."

The fifteen-year-old hangs up. I dial a florist.

"I need a corsage. It's an emergency."

"It's almost five o'clock," the lady at the florist's says.

"I know, but this is really important. I'm taking this girl to the prom tomorrow, and she's going to expect a corsage."

"We'll see what we can do."

At 5:25 I stop at the florist's.

"Hi, I called about the corsage. Is it ready?"

"We did make up a corsage," the lady says, "but we're holding it for a young man who needs one to give to his date for the prom."

"That's me. I called about half an hour ago."

It takes a while, but finally I convince the lady that I am

the one who needs the corsage to give to his date for the high school prom. I give her $6.50. She gives me the corsage. And a list of four singles bars where I can go to meet women my own age.

On the day of the prom, I shine my shoes, comb my hair, put on my tuxedo, and look at my reflection in the mirror. This will be my third prom. But it will be the first without a pimple on my chin.

By seven o'clock everybody gathers at our house. The fifteen-year-old is lovely. Karen is lovely. Bruce is handsome. I am starting to get a pimple on my chin. We take a lot of snapshots. The fifteen-year-old and me. Karen and me. The fifteen-year-old and Bruce. In hundreds of homes all over town, this same scene is being repeated. But ours may be the only one in which the wife is taking pictures of her husband and his teenage date.

We drive to the restaurant where Bruce has made reservations. The maître d' says there will be a short wait, but we are welcome to sit in the lounge. Bruce and the fifteen-year-old sit together and order Cokes. The bartender turns to where Karen and I are sitting together. She doesn't want anything.

"How about you, Roman Polanski?" he smirks.

"I'll have a Shirley Temple. Easy on the grenadine."

After dinner we drive to the prom, where we dance until midnight. As far as I can see, the only difference between the way Karen and I dance and the other couples dance is that, on slow songs, we actually move our feet.

At midnight we drive to the after-prom. A battalion of chaperones is stationed at the entrance to make sure no unauthorized persons, beverages, or smoking matter makes it inside.

One of the chaperones looks up as I walk in.

"You're late," she says. "Chaperones were supposed to be here an hour ago."

"I'm not a chaperone. I'm Karen's date."

"Aren't you a little old for high school."

"I keep flunking geometry."

When the after-prom is over, we drive around until we find a place that is open where we can find something to eat. It is 5:30 in the morning. I'm feeling fine. But the fifteen-year-old's head is resting on Bruce's shoulder, and Karen is resting her chin on her arms.

Next year, I resolve, I'm going to have to find a younger group to go to the prom with.

Having survived the prom, I have no reason to suspect that taking our daughter on a trip should be much of a problem. So when she is sixteen, I take her on a trip to New York City as her Christmas present.

The way I figure it, sixteen is the perfect age to introduce her to the Big Apple. I am going to be there on business anyway, and it will be easy to take her along and show her the diversity of one of the world's most remarkable cities. From the tackiness of Times Square to the elegance of Lincoln Center. From the dignified opulence of the Waldorf-Astoria to the hectic clamor of Chinatown. It will be a tremendously educational trip for her. If nothing else, it will give her something to think about besides boys for a few days.

So we fly to New York City and we check in at the Waldorf-Astoria, which is one of the world's classiest hotels. I realize it is one of the world's classiest hotels when I show up at the registration desk with a sixteen-year-old girl and the clerk never changes expressions. For a moment, I am tempted to test his cool by registering as Hugh Hefner. But the urge passes and I sign my real name: Humbert Humbert.

That evening we go to Lincoln Center to see an opera.

The sixteen-year-old fidgets through the first act of the opera. At intermission she mentions that she is not enthralled with the performance. As nearly as I can recall, her exact words are: "If I have to sit through one more minute of this grody junk I'm gonna barf my guts out."

"All right," I tell her, "there's a couch in the lower lobby. You can sit there and wait for me during the second act. But don't blame me if you're bored silly."

I watch the second half of the opera alone. When it is over, I return to the lower lobby. The sixteen-year-old still is on the couch. She does not look bored silly. Neither does the nineteen-year-old usher who is seated next to her.

"The opera's over and thousands of people are trying to find the exits without your help," I mention to him. The usher mumbles something to the sixteen-year-old and walks back to resume ushing. We take a cab back to the hotel.

The next day I take her for a subway ride. We get off at Houston Street and wander around through Greenwich Village, Little Italy, and Chinatown. This is what New York is all about: ethnic groups, their distinctive cultures mingling in colorful and picturesque harmony. This is what I brought her to see.

We walk into an Oriental grocery store filled with unusual items. I point out some of them to her: dried fungus, braised bamboo shoots, sugar cane juice.

"Look at this strange stuff," I say. "It looks like some kind of dried fish. I wonder what it is?"

There is no answer. I turn around. The reason there is no answer is because she is no longer standing next to me. She is on the other side of the store, talking to a teenage Chinese stockboy. I'm not sure what he is saying, but he is trying to get her to accept a box of lychee nuts.

We leave the store and take a subway back to Times Square. She decides that she needs a souvenir T-shirt from Times Square to take back home. We stop at a store that has roughly five million T-shirts in stock. She wants to look at each one.

"Listen, I'm not going to stand in this joint all day while you read T-shirts," I tell her. "I'll be out front."

I walk out of the store and stand on Broadway, amazed at the passing parade of weirdos, crazies, and perverts you always see around Times Square. But after half an hour I grow tired of watching tourists. I go back inside to see what's keeping the sixteen-year-old.

She is talking to a sales clerk. He has dark hair and bristly whiskers and he's wearing a dark suit with no tie. He looks familiar. I think I've seen pictures of him on the news. Holding up signs in front of the U.S. Embassy in Tehran.

"Hey, mister," he says, "would you mind if I took out your daughter tonight?"

I tell him what he can do with his oil and we leave the souvenir shop.

The last thing on our agenda is a cocktail party. We go to the party. I walk to the bar for a drink. When I return, the sixteen-year-old is surrounded by three kids from Great Neck. I know they're three kids from Great Neck because when I walk up to them, the tallest one says, "Hi, we're three kids from Great Neck."

They hang around us for the rest of the party. When it is time to leave, they follow us outside.

"We'll help you get a cab," one of them says. He hails a cab. It stops. I open the rear door on the driver's side and we pile in: me, the sixteen-year-old, and the three kids from Great Neck. At precisely the same moment, someone opens the rear door on the other side. A girl and a guy pile in.

"This is our cab," the guy says.

I start to get out.

"No it isn't," says one of the kids with us. "We had it first."

"Maybe we should let them have the cab," I tell the kid. "We can walk back to the hotel. It can't be more than thirty or forty blocks."

"Hey, no way," the kid says, "I'm not letting this creep push us around."

They argue back and forth while the cab sits there in the middle of the street. The only thing moving is the meter. Eventually a compromise is reached. The cab will drop us off at the hotel and then take the guy and his date to wherever they are going. The cab begins to move. One of the kids makes another smart remark to the guy. He takes exception. He threatens to beat the stuffing out of the kid. And his two friends. And the old guy.

"What old guy?" I ask the sixteen-year-old.

"I think he means you."

It is the longest five-dollar cab ride in the history of New York, but eventually we arrive at our hotel. We get out with our stuffing still inside of us and walk into the lobby. Me and the sixteen-year-old and the three kids from Great Neck.

Two hours later we finally get rid of them. We go up to the room and I collapse onto my bed. It has been a hectic trip. In two days I have fended off an AWOL usher, a Chinese lychee-nut pusher, Bani-Sadr's nephew, and three kids from Great Neck. The visit to New York has not turned out exactly the way I envisioned it. On the other hand, it's been years since I've seen her get this much enjoyment out of a Christmas present.

But sixteen is not just the year she makes a serious commitment to boy-meeting. It also is the year she learns to drive. It is not a moment I have been looking forward to with all my heart and soul. The problem is that I can remember other years.

I remember when she is nine and she asks me if she can push the grocery cart at the store.

I say yes.

She runs it into six other carts, a cardboard cutout of Mr. Whipple squeezing his Charmin, three cash registers, a peanut-butter display, and a fat lady in hot pants.

And I remember when she is thirteen and she asks me if she can cut the grass with the rider mower.

I say yes.

She drives it over four tomato plants, a lazy dog, a quick brown fox, thirty feet of split-rail fence, a bird bath, and a very angry, wet sparrow.

Unfortunately, remembering these things does not prevent her from wanting to learn how to drive a car. So on the day she turns sixteen, she comes to me and asks if I will take her to get her temporary driver's license.

And I say: "You've got to be kidding. Did Machine Gun Kelly's father take him to buy ammunition? After what you did with the rider mower, you don't really think I'm going to turn you loose with a car."

"I don't know why you keep bringing that up," she says. "That was three years ago. Besides, I already explained that the only reason I hit those things was because I couldn't remember which pedal was for the gas and which was for the other thing."

"The brake."

"Yeah. That's the one."

"How about explaining why you also hit two of your brothers."

"The other one kept dodging."

"Well, I don't really think you're ready to start driving a car. So let's just forget about it for now. And don't make that face. My mind is made up and that's it. There's no possible way I'm going to agree to letting you get your driver's license right now. F. Lee Bailey could not talk me into changing my decision. Case closed."

That evening, the woman who promised to love, honor, and bang my gavel reopens the case. She points out that she thinks it would be a terrific idea if the sixteen-year-old got her license.

"Why in the world would you want her to get her license?" I demand.

"Why not? I think she'll be a very good driver."

"Good driver? Remember when she got her Big Wheel? She had so many accidents on it our insurance company raised our rates. She's the only kid I ever saw who needed to wear a crash helmet when she was operating the vacuum cleaner."

"She's matured a lot since then. Anyway, if she has a license, it will save us lots of hassles."

"What hassles?"

"For instance, when I'm busy she can drive in the car pool."

"I don't care. It's not worth it."

"She can drive to the store for groceries."

"She's just too young."

"She can take the eight-year-old to Cub Scout meetings. That way you won't have to take him."

"Tell her to sign up for driver's education tomorrow."

For the next few months, the sixteen-year-old takes driver's education at school. When she finishes the course, she announces that she is ready to take her test.

"How can you be ready?" I ask. "The only car you've ever driven is the one at school. You're going to have to get really used to our car before you can use it for the driver's test. That means you need a great deal more driving time with a competent, patient, experienced adult."

"OK, how about if I do some practice driving this afternoon?" she asks.

"Good idea. You go out and get into the car. Your mother will be out in a minute."

Unfortunately, the woman who promised to love, honor, and rotate my tires has heard the whole conversation. I know she has heard the whole conversation, because she has disappeared. I am going to have to go out with the sixteen-year-old myself.

I get into the car on the passenger's side.

"Start it up, pull it out of the garage, down the driveway and into the street," I say.

She starts it up, backs it out of the garage, down the driveway and into the street. In 2.3 seconds. When the car is in the street, she glances at me.

"Why are you whimpering?" she asks. "Did I do something wrong?"

"No, no. That was fine. The fifty-five-mile-an-hour speed limit probably doesn't apply to driveways, anyway."

We drive around the block onto the main drag and then out into the flow of highway traffic. Actually, she proves to be a pretty good driver, and after a few miles I settle back and relax. Toward the end of the drive I even open my eyes.

After several weeks of practice, she takes her driver's test. She becomes a fully licensed driver, permitted to drive everywhere. I am sure she will be quite competent.

Her brothers, on the other hand, aren't turning their backs

on her. And there's a sparrow in the backyard who won't go near the birdbath when she's behind the wheel.

Despite the assurances of the woman who promised to love, honor, and fill my air bag, letting the sixteen-year-old get her driver's license does not save us lots of hassles. It just creates new and more terrifying hassles. There is, for instance, the day I ask her to pick up her brother after his football practice.

By now she has her own car, a gift from her maternal grandmother, who never did like me very much.

"I can't pick him up," the sixteen-year-old says, "my car's out of gas."

"Again?"

"I don't understand it," she admits. "I put a dollar's worth in it just last week."

"Well then, take your mother's."

"She took it to the store."

"All right, take my MG Midget. It's running this week."

"I don't know how to drive it, remember? It has a stick shift and they don't use cars with stick shifts in driver's education."

"I can't believe it. When I was in school, all the cars they used for driver's education had manual transmissions."

"When you were in school, all the cars had rumble seats."

That weekend I decide that it is time for her to learn how to drive a car with a manual transmission. So I take her out to the garage, put her behind the wheel of my MG Midget, show her the clutch, and point out the little diagram on the top of the floor shift.

"There's nothing to it," I tell her. "To back it out of the garage, you have to do five things: push in the clutch, turn the key, slip it into reverse, step on the gas, and ease out the clutch."

She does those five things. But not in that order. As she grinds it into reverse, a sound of metallic pain comes from deep inside the car. The last time I heard a sound like that was when the five-year-old decided to throw away his Matchbox model cars. In the garbage disposal.

When the clanging has subsided, she looks at me.

"I must have done something wrong," she says.

"I never like to use a negative word like 'wrong.' Let's just say that, over the years, many drivers have reached the conclusion that it's easier to shift gears when the clutch is in."

She tries again. This time she gets the car into reverse.

"OK, now slowly step on the gas while at the same time easing out the clutch pedal."

Her right foot gently touches the gas pedal. Her left foot pops up as if the clutch pedal is radioactive. The car lurches three feet backward and dies.

"That wasn't good, was it?" she asks.

"Well, at least we're moving in the right direction. Try again."

She tries again. The car lurches backward three more feet. I lean over and look at the dashboard.

"What are you looking for?" she asks.

"Just checking to see if we have enough gas to get out of the driveway."

On her third try, she gets the car out of the garage. As we roll down the driveway to the street, I tell her, "When we get into the street, shift from reverse into first gear."

We get into the street. She shifts from reverse into first gear. Without stopping in-between. When all four wheels are back on the ground, I turn to her.

"What the heck were the names of the driving teachers you had in school, Starsky and Hutch?"

Ignoring me, she whips it into second, leaving a little patch of rubber behind on the street.

"This is fun, " she says, slamming it down into third. She has one hand on the wheel, one hand on the gear shift, a smile on her lips, and a sparkle in her eyes. And, in my stomach, gears are grinding. I have a terrible feeling that, once upon a time,

Mr. Knievel said to his son, "How about picking up your brother at football practice, Evel?"

Somehow she manages to survive a year of offensive driving and turn seventeen. Which means another birthday party.

When she was little, her birthday parties were simple affairs. There was a cake, some ice cream, and a quick chorus of "Happy Birthday." The whole thing took maybe fifteen minutes, from the lighting of the first candle to the breaking of the last present.

As she gets older, she expects more. Little friends have to be invited for the party. Games have to be played. Token gifts have to be bought for each little guest, so that no kid will be without a present to break.

Eventually she reaches the point where parties at home are no longer enough. To be successful, the birthday party has to go on the road.

The first year it is just a couple of kids, and we take them to a movie. The next year it has escalated to half a dozen kids, and the movie is followed by a trip to the pizza place. On her sixteenth birthday there are ten kids, and the movie and pizza are followed by two hours at the skating rink.

All of which has me breathless with anticipation as we approach her seventeenth birthday.

"Let me guess," I say when the subject is brought up by the woman who promised to love, honor, and blow out my candles. "This year she wants us to take the entire junior class to a Broadway play, fly to Paris for dinner at Maxim's, rent the Astrodome for three nights of . . ."

"She wants to have a party at home."

"She does? That's terrific."

"What's so terrific about it? Don't you remember the last time she had a party at home?"

"Oh, yeah. I guess that did get a little out of hand."

"The Iranian revolution got a little out of hand. That party was a major disaster."

"Oh, it wasn't all that bad."

"No? Then how come we have the only homeowner's insurance policy I've ever seen that won't pay off in the event of war, acts of God, or teenage parties?"

"I'll talk to her about it."

I talk to her about it. She convinces me that this time the party will be a little different. By which I assume that she means this time the party will not include a rock band, twenty-five rock-band groupies, the football team, a motorcycle gang, or the police force.

I report back to the woman who promised to love, honor, and drive the paddy wagon.

"It shouldn't be too bad," I say. "She's only having fourteen kids, and they'll be out of the house by midnight. And she promises that they'll all stay in the rec room the whole night."

"That sounds awful," she says. "What could be worse than fourteen teenagers making noise all night in the rec room?"

"Fourteen teenagers being quiet all night in the rec room."

So we agree to let her have the party, and shortly after eight o'clock the following Saturday, a loud burst of noise explodes out of the rec room.

"What was that?" I ask the woman who promised to love, honor, and clean my seismograph.

"The party's starting. She just turned on the stereo down there."

"Thank God. I was afraid the furnace blew up."

The party lasts almost fifteen minutes before the first teenage faces appear in our living room. It is the seventeen-year-old and one of her girlfriends.

"What are you doing up here?" I demand. "You promised that you'd stay down in the rec room."

"She cut herself," the seventeen-year-old says, pointing to where a trickle of blood is running down her girlfriend's forehead.

"How did she do that?"

"She bumped into the hall light."

"But the hall light is on the ceiling."

"I know. She was just walking down the stairs and sort of bumped into it."

I think about that. The ceiling fixture is nine feet above the floor. The girl's forehead is five and a half feet above the floor. If she was just walking down the stairs and she sort of bumped into it, there's only one thing to do. Get her a tryout for the National Basketball Association.

We patch up the girl's forehead, make her promise not to try anymore slam dunks for the rest of the evening, and send them both back downstairs. A short time later, I go downstairs, too. Just to make sure they're not out of pretzels or anything.

Fourteen barefoot teenagers are scattered throughout the rec room, and a pile of shoes is in the corner. One of the many mysteries of parenthood is how a teenager can go barefoot 95 percent of her life and still manage to wear out twenty-three pairs of shoes a year.

Two barefoot couples are playing pool. One barefoot couple is sitting on a chair. The rest are dancing to a record on the stereo. At least I assume it's a record. It could be a tape recording of World War II.

The party lasts until midnight. When it is over, six cases of pop have been drunk, eight pounds of potato chips have been eaten, twelve pounds of potato chips have been ground into the carpet, three faces have been smeared with birthday-cake frosting, four romances have ended, six romances have started, and one teenage boy has been discovered sitting in a tree in the front yard.

Next year, I vow, I'm going to try to talk her into letting us take the senior class to a Broadway play, flying to Paris for dinner at Maxim's, renting the Astrodome for three nights of . . .

But birthday parties prove to be the least of my problems in the next year. Because before she can turn eighteen, a letter arrives at our house that I instantly realize is going to introduce us to a new era of poverty.

"Dear Ms. Stewart," the letter begins. "We are pleased to inform you that you have been accepted for admission at the University. Please arrange to have your father's paychecks forwarded directly to us for the next four years."

The woman who promised to love, honor, and carry my books greets the news with enthusiasm.

"Just think," she says, "in a few months she'll be packing her bags and heading off for one of the greatest adventures of her life. Isn't that wonderful?"

"Let's see how wonderful you think it is when you find out that what she's packing her bags with is most of your favorite clothes."

"You certainly don't seem very pleased about this whole thing," she notes.

"Well, sure, I'm pleased. It's just that I'm concerned about how we're going to pay for it. Do you have any idea what it costs to send a kid to college these days? I read somewhere that a private school runs something like $7,000 a year. Where's that money going to come from?"

"You mean you haven't saved for it?"

"How was I supposed to know that she was going to grow up?"

"That's ridiculous. You knew this day would come eventually. You should have been ready for it."

"To tell the truth, I was hoping that she'd win a scholarship that would take care of it all."

"Winning a scholarship is pretty tough."

"Oh, I don't know. The kid up the street won a full four-year scholarship to the same school she's going to. Why couldn't she have done something like that?"

"Because the kid up the street weighs 275 pounds and won a football scholarship."

"Is it my fault she didn't spend more time on her pass blocking?"

"Well, let's not worry about it right now. I'm sure we'll come up with the money somehow."

She's right, I guess. Still, it's another financial worry. And it's not eased any by the seventeen-year-old, who bursts into the room a few minutes later.

"Did you hear the news?" she asks.

"Yes. Congratulations. I'm very happy for you."

"Good. When can we go shopping?"

"Shopping?"

"You know. For the things I'm going to need at college."

"Slow down. You've got six months to go yet. Besides, you can't buy the things you'll need at college until you find out exactly what courses you'll be taking. After you register for classes, they'll tell you exactly which books and supplies you'll need."

"I wasn't talking about books and supplies, exactly."

"You said the things you need for college."

"I meant, like, a refrigerator for my room in the dorm."

"You won't need a refrigerator. They feed you in the cafeteria. That's why we pay room and board."

"But *nobody* eats in the cafeteria. Everybody has refrigerators in their rooms so they can keep food there."

"Well, if everybody has a refrigerator, you can just share the one your roommate will be bringing."

"I thought of that. But what if she's a big fat girl who keeps so much food in there for herself that I won't be able to get any of my stuff into it? Then I won't have anyplace to put my food and it will spoil and I'll get botulism and spend my first semester in the infirmary and get incompletes in all my classes and get thrown out of school and drift aimlessly around the country and wind up in Southern California and shave my head and join a commune with a group of anarchists. I think I read somewhere that Squeaky Fromme's father wouldn't buy her a refrigerator for her dorm room."

I'm not sure what she's going to be majoring in at college. But I hope it's logic.

"OK, OK," I say, "I'll think about the refrigerator. What else are you going to need?"

"Well, a stereo, for sure. And a television, so I don't have to miss "General Hospital." And, probably, a new car, because I don't think my old one will be able to get me back and forth on weekends. And, I'll really need . . .

Her list goes on and on, but I really don't pay much attention. I'm busy trying to add up the cost of a refrigerator so that she won't have to eat the cafeteria food I'll be paying for, a television so she'll have something to do instead of sitting in the classes I'll be paying for, and a car so she won't have to spend too much time in the dormitory room I'll be paying for.

Eventually I give up. I never was very good at math. But I have an idea I'm going to learn. I think her college is going to give me a real education.

# 4

## MY TUB RUNNETH OVER

When we built our dream house, the woman who promised to love, honor, and live there happily ever after walked around it a few times and said, "It's nice . . . but the yard sure looks bare."

So I went to the garden center and spent a small fortune, and soon we had grass and shrubs and flowers and skinny little maple trees that one day will grow into handsome large maple trees. About twenty years after I am dead.

The winter after we moved into our dream house, the woman who promised to love, honor, and keep me busy sat in the living room and said, "It's nice . . . but it sure would be great if the kids had some place roomy to play when the weather is too nasty for them to go outside."

So I went to the home–improvement center and spent a large fortune, and soon we had a basement with paneling on the walls and tiles on the ceiling and carpet on the floor and stereo speakers on shelves so records could be played down there by the kids. All four of whom prefer to play in their bedrooms.

When the following summer came to our dream house, the

woman who promised to love, honor, and keep my cash flowing stood in the family room and looked out into the backyard and said, "It's nice . . . but it sure would be terrific if we had an outside area for entertaining."

So I went to the hardware store and spent two large fortunes, and soon we had a large concrete patio, with a redwood picnic table and folding chaise lounges, and a white aluminum patio cover to keep you dry when it's raining. If you know where to sit.

Seven years after we moved into our dream house, the woman who promised to love, honor, and prune my limbs walked through the yard and saw the maturing bushes and trees. She walked down to the basement and saw the spacious rec room with the thick carpeting and the large pool table. She looked out at the patio, built to accommodate 700 or 800 of our dearest friends.

And she said, "Let's move."

"You're kidding," I say.

"No I'm not," she says. "This place is getting old."

"Seven years does not exactly qualify a house to be put on the National Register of Historic Places," I point out.

"Maybe not. But I think it's a good idea to move out now before all the things that are wearing out completely fall apart."

"Like what?"

"Like the downstairs shower."

"What are you talking about? We don't have a downstairs shower."

"We will, just as soon as the floor in the upstairs bathroom caves in from the water flooding over on it all the time."

"If you wouldn't let the thirteen-year-old take two-hour showers, we wouldn't have that problem. The last time he took a shower up there, he sang Beatles' songs."

"So?"

"All of them."

"Anyway," she says, "the shower's not the only thing wrong. The upstairs toilet won't shut off and every faucet in the house drips and the gutters and downspouts are all dented from being hit by basketballs and the family room shag carpet is bald and all the walls need painting."

"That covers just about everything but the kitchen sink," I admit.

"That's another thing. Look in the kitchen sink and tell me what you see."

"Two dirty Star Wars glasses and a knife with half a pound of peanut butter still on it."

"I mean under that."

"I don't see anything."

"You're just not trying. What about those two big chunks missing out of it?"

"Chunks? I don't see any chunks. All I see are the two tiny little chips that are practically invisible to the naked eye."

"The diamond you bought me when we got engaged is a tiny little chip that is practically invisible to the naked eye. Those things are chunks."

"Well, hang on and I'll call an engineer and see how long he thinks the house can survive that kind of structural damage."

"Go ahead, make jokes," she says. "It's obvious that you are not going to worry about me spending the rest of my life here in this death trap, never knowing when a floor is going to collapse or the plumbing is going to explode or one of the kids is going to be electrocuted by wiring that probably was installed by Thomas Edison. One good thing, I suppose, is that the doorbell doesn't work. So when the Board of Health comes out to condemn . . ."

"All right, all right, we'll sell the stupid house."

That evening I hear her on the phone, talking to a real estate agent about selling our house.

" . . . that's right, as soon as possible," she says. "The condition of this house? Oh, it's practically brand-new."

The next thing I know, our house is for sale. There is a big sign out front, and every day people come to look at it, strangers who walk slowly from room to room, passing judgment on our ability to hang wallpaper, poking curiously through the last seven years of our lives.

They listen politely as the real estate agent tells them the good things about our house, frowning slightly when her glowing words do not quite agree with the slightly worn evidence before their eyes.

"The family room has a fireplace and a lovely shag rug," she tells them, leading them that way.

And there is a shag rug in the family room. But it's a tired shag, matted down a bit from hours spent wrestling and roughhousing and playing Stewart ball on it. These people probably never heard of Stewart ball. It's a silly game, really, with no equipment but a Nerf ball and no real rules, only lots of running and tickling and little boys jumping on their father's stomach. We don't play Stewart ball anymore. The little boys are getting too old. Their father is getting too busy.

Anyway, these people aren't interested in Stewart ball. They want to know about interest rates and loan assumptions and average monthly heating bills. So the real estate agent tells them what they want to know as she guides them through the kitchen, where there is a stove that is a veteran of 10,000 pans of macaroni and cheese and a refrigerator that has survived ten times as many openings.

"It has four bedrooms and two baths up," she announces, leading them up the stairs.

"This bedroom's pretty small," the man whispers to his wife as they stand in the hall looking in.

They're right, I guess. That bedroom is pretty small.

But it was just the right size for the tiny little boy we brought home from the hospital five years ago. There was just enough room for a crib to put him in and a bassinet to change him on and a rocking chair for his mother to sit in while she held him close to her heart and nursed him in the warm, still silence of a summer night.

The couple follows the real estate lady to another bedroom

and, even before he says it, I know he's thinking that these walls will have to be painted if they buy the house.

And they will, too, because they're spotted with thumbtack holes and Scotch-tape marks and other proof that two little boys spent a lot of rainy afternoons in here.

We probably should have used more foresight and not let the walls get that way. But how do you say no when an eight-year-old Cub Scout comes home with a gold ribbon to hang above his bed that proclaims him the third best rope climber in his entire den? How can you not tape up a five-year-old's family portrait, made with love and fingerpaint, showing that Dad is as tall as a house and Mom has beautiful yellow hair and his big brother looks like the Incredible Hulk?

The sixteen-year-old's bedroom, that will need painting, too. Somehow, these people don't look like the kind who would want a gray bedroom streaked with hand-painted horizontal stripes and geometric designs. It probably looks strange to them. It certainly looked strange to us when we saw what she had done.

But it was just the right kind of a room for a young lady to go and hide in when the confusion of adolescence chipped away at the security of childhood. It was just the right kind of place to discover Led Zeppelin and feathered hair and phone conversations that rambled pointlessly into the evening.

The outside of our house isn't perfect, either. The gutter that runs across the front of the garage roof is twisted and ruptured, a victim of seasons of basketballs that just missed the rim hanging over the driveway.

And when the people walk into the backyard, they'll see that there are bare spots in the crabgrass. If they look closely enough, they'll see that the barest spots are where the bases on a softball diamond would be, a diamond that attracted every kid in the neighborhood on hot and drowsy afternoons. And the biggest kid of all was the all-time pitcher, who would lay 'em in there for hours, or until his wife called out through the patio door to tell him that his office was on the phone and they were just wondering if his Tuesday column was done yet.

A lot of things about this house aren't perfect anymore. Too many things, perhaps, for these people to be interested in it. It's hard to tell as they walk back to the driveway and thank the real estate agent and get into their car and drive away.

Maybe they'll be back. Or maybe they'll decide that too many walls need painting, too many areas of the shag carpet are worn and matted, too much living has taken place here.

It's not, after all, the greatest house in town. But it's been a pretty good home.

Finally we find a family willing to buy our house full of memories, and it is time to move out.

In Robert Young's world, moving out of a house would be a momentous event. It would be square-jawed moving men with bulging muscles and sparkling white uniforms carefully carrying out the Anderson family's treasures and loading them into shining vans. It would be a flurry of activity, a farewell party from the neighbors, a funny feeling in the pit of his stomach as he looks back for one last glance at the house where so much happened in his life.

Of course, that's in Robert Young's world.

In the real world, moving out of a house is lukewarm leftover spaghetti. Eaten with a spoon.

I tried to tell the woman who promised to love, honor, and label my boxes that it would be that way, but she didn't believe me.

"Moving will be a snap," she says. "All we have to do is get a couple of those square-jawed guys with bulging muscles and sparkling white uniforms."

"By the time we come up with the money for the down payment on a new house, we're not going to have enough money left over to hire an emaciated hippie in greasy overalls," I point out. "We're going to have to do the moving ourselves."

So I make arrangements to borrow a pickup truck, line up some guys to help me carry the big stuff, and get ready for the move. On the night before we leave, the neighbors throw an enormous party. It is one of the biggest parties ever held on our street. I only wish we had been invited.

The next afternoon I leave work early, get the pickup truck, and drive home. The woman who promised to love, honor, and carry the washing machine is not there. She has gone ahead to clean the new house. I am not quite sure why it is necessary to clean a house that never has been lived in, but she insists that it's important.

I have about half an hour until the guys who are going to help me move show up. It should be just enough time to put together some lunch. I go to the refrigerator. It is practically empty, which means one of two things: either she has cleaned it out and moved the food to the new house, or the sixteen-year-old's boyfriend was just here. The only things left are a Tupperware bowl full of cooked spaghetti with no sauce, half an orange, and a bottle of Mexican hot sauce.

I consider the possibilities. I could put the hot sauce on the spaghetti and eat the orange for dessert. I could put the orange on the spaghetti and eat the hot sauce for dessert. I could put the hot sauce on the orange and eat the spaghetti for dessert. I could phone out for a pizza.

I take the bowl of spaghetti to the stove and pull open the drawer in which we keep all of our pots and pans. The drawer is empty. She has taken our pans to the new house. Both of them. The only cooking container left behind is the tea kettle. It sounds like an awful lot of work to get the spaghetti into it.

Instead, I heat some water in the tea kettle and pour it over the bowl of cold spaghetti. It is a terrific idea. In just a few minutes I have a bowl of soggy spaghetti. In hot water.

All I have to do now is separate the hot water from the soggy spaghetti, a simple task ordinarily performed with the aid of a colander. Which she has taken with her to the new house. The best I can do is pour off as much of the water as I can. Carefully, I drain the water into the sink. When I have finished,

I have half a bowl of watery spaghetti lying there like a family of albino nightcrawlers after a hard rain.

I return to the refrigerator. Nothing has grown in it in the last fifteen minutes. I take out the Mexican hot sauce and pour a couple of ounces on top of the spaghetti. I carry the bowl to the silverware drawer to get a fork.

The silverware drawer is empty.

Not only has she cleaned out the knives, forks, and spoons, she also has taken the potato peeler, the can opener, the rubber bands, the marbles, the dog's expired license, and the broken pencils.

Eventually I locate a spoon, which was left behind in the back of the dishwashing machine. By now the spaghetti is down to lukewarm and is plunging toward cold again. The Mexican hot sauce has mixed with the water. I haven't seen a liquid that color since the last time I drained my radiator.

I sit down in the middle of the kitchen floor to slurp my lukewarm spaghetti and Mexican hot sauce with a spoon. This will be, I realize, my very last meal in this house where so much has happened in my life. Thinking about it, I get a funny feeling in the pit of my stomach. I'm betting it's indigestion.

If there is any consolation in all of this, it is that soon I will be in our new house, sitting in my Jacuzzi.

Most of my life I have lived in places that had bathtubs just big enough for me, a sliver of soap, and one small toy boat. Some day, I would promise myself as I sat in hip-high water with my knees tucked up under my chin, I will have a tub so big that I will be able to sink down in bubbles up to my chin without dangling my legs over the end.

Finally, I have met the tub of my dreams. Actually, I am fixed up with it on a blind date by the woman who promised to love, honor, and scrub my back. She discovers it in the course of house-hunting.

"I've found just the place for us," she says. "You're going to love it. It has five bedrooms."

"Terrific. That will give each kid a floor of his own to throw his clothes on."

"It has a built-in microwave oven."

"So we won't have to wait as long for dinner to be ruined."

"And it has a large fireplace," she continues, undeterred.

"You know how I feel about fireplaces. I couldn't get a fire going in one of those things with two cords of wood, twelve gallons of kerosene, a mile of faulty wiring, and ten kids playing with matches."

"But, best of all," she says, pausing for effect, "it has a Jacuzzi."

"We already have a dog."

"A Jacuzzi isn't a dog. It's a bathtub. A giant bathtub with an electric motor that creates soothing streams of water that will just bubble your worries away."

"Well, I suppose we could take a look at the place."

The next day we take a look at the place. As advertised, it has five bedrooms, a microwave, and a fireplace. And, in the master bedroom, there is an enormous built-in bathtub with carpeted steps leading up to it and dark brown tile surrounding it on three sides.

"Think you could be comfortable in that?" the real estate man asks.

"Moby Dick could be comfortable in that," I admit.

So we buy the house and move all of our belongings into it. And while all of our belongings still are stacked in crates in the living room and the Mexican hot sauce stains still are on my chin, I take a bottle of bubble bath, a mug of hot tea, and a copy of *The Rise and Fall of the Third Reich* and head for the Jacuzzi.

I turn on the water full blast and begin to undress. By the time I am down to my freckles, there is perhaps half an inch of water on the bottom of the tub. I sit down, turn to page one of my book, and wait for the tub to be full enough for me to get into it.

In the time it takes the water level to be high enough for

me to get in, Hitler is born, serves in World War I, goes to prison, writes *Mein Kampf*, comes to power, and annexes three countries.

But at last the water level is high enough, and I am in a tub that is bigger than I am. I stretch out, luxuriating in water that is up around my shoulders. After a few minutes of soaking, I decide that it is time to try the motor that creates soothing streams of water that will just bubble my worries away.

Spaced around the inside of the tub at different levels are the openings through which the electric motor forces the streams of water. Before turning on the motor, the Jacuzzi manual cautions, the water level must be above all six of the openings. I check to make sure that the water level is above all six of the openings. It is. I check to see if I can turn on the motor. I can't.

This is because the control that turns on the motor is located on a wall six feet from the tub. The only way to reach it is to get out of the tub.

I get out of the tub, leaving neat little puddles of water on the carpeted steps. I turn on the control. Behind me, I hear a rumbling sound. Followed by the sensation of water hitting me in the back. Getting out of the tub has lowered the water level. Instead of forcing streams of water below the surface, the Jacuzzi is shooting water all over the bathroom like a drunken fireman.

Water is bouncing off the walls, off the ceiling, off the mirror. In this moment of crisis, I do what I do best. I panic.

Frantically, I turn the control. The wrong way. The Jacuzzi now is programmed to run for an hour. The way I figure it, an hour of this and the master bedroom is going to be floating past the large fireplace. The only way to stop the deluge is to raise the water level in the tub. In a desperate leap for the tub, I do a one–and–a–half with a twist and hit the water. Except for my left knee, which hits the edge of the tub. The water sloshes back and forth for a while, then settles down.

Finally the Jacuzzi is working the way it is supposed to. The motor is rumbling beneath me, sending out streams of water through the six openings. The water is agitating around me. It is like sitting inside a dishwasher.

Sitting there, I can see water dripping from the newly plastered ceiling. I can see little puddles of water soaking into the carpet. I can see my left knee turning purple. I can imagine the water meter working overtime to calculate the cost of filling this tub.

Fortunately, I have this Jacuzzi to bubble away my worries.

# 5

## VIDEO GAMES

The happiness in our home lasts until shortly after the moment the kids first discover the green edges around Sheriff Lobo.

"They're driving me crazy with their complaining about the television," says the woman who promised to love, honor, and turn my dial. "You're going to have to do something about it."

I walk into the living room, where the thirteen-year-old is sitting on the floor in front of the television. By his grim and unsmiling expression, I assume he is watching "Laverne & Shirley."

"Your mother says there's some sort of problem with the television."

"There sure is, Dad. The reception is terrible. Just look at the picture."

I look at the picture. If I squint my eyes just right, I can see a vague outline of a green person wearing a shirt stretched so tightly across the chest that it obviously is going to rip apart at any moment.

"The picture's not as good as it should be," I agree. "On the other hand, I don't think you're missing too much if you don't see every little detail of the "Incredible Hulk.""

"That's not the Incredible Hulk, Dad. It's Dolly Parton."

"Well, let's try another channel."

He turns the dial. On the next channel, we see several figures walking in a snowstorm.

"Nothing wrong with that picture," I point out. "You can see quite clearly that there are a bunch of people walking in a blizzard. By the way, what's the name of that show?"

"Aloha, Paradise."

"OK, so maybe the picture is not the best in the world. But that's because we don't have an antenna on the roof here. But I really don't feel like going through all that hassle of installing one. When I did it at the old house, I had to crawl on my hands and knees through insulation in the attic that stuck in my skin for weeks. Then I had to climb out onto the roof and make holes in the chimney to attach the antenna supports. It was a real project."

"That doesn't sound so bad to me."

"It probably wouldn't have been if I'd had a drill. Just wait until you're the father and you have to make holes in a brick chimney with a hammer and a bent nail."

"I don't know what you're complaining about, Dad. I'm the one who had to always climb out through the bedroom window to turn the antenna every time we changed channels because you couldn't figure out how to hook up the rotor."

"Well, I don't want either of us to go through that again. So let's just settle for a fuzzy picture."

"We don't have to settle for that, Dad. We could get cable. Everybody else on the block has it. It's neat, too. Because you get a lot of channels from other cities."

"Terrific. Instead of "Love Boat" reruns and a lot of stupid local commercials, we can have "Love Boat" reruns and a bunch of stupid out-of-town commercials."

"But they've got a lot of other great things," he persists.

"They have all-sports channels and all-movie channels. They even have an all-news channel. Imagine being able to get the news whenever you want instead of having to wait until six or eleven."

"What will they think of next?" I say, laying aside my newspaper.

That evening I mention to the woman who promised to love, honor, and turn my dial that the thirteen-year-old is pushing for cable TV.

"I think it's a good idea," she says. "They have a lot of educational channels we can't get now."

"I'm sorry. I just don't think that we can afford it right now with the new house payments. Besides, more channels just means that they would waste more of their time watching television instead of going out each day to till and plant and harvest the crops the way I did when I was a boy."

"What are you talking about? You grew up in the middle of Cleveland."

"Yeah, but we had window boxes. Real big ones. Anyway, that's all beside the point. I just don't think we really need cable TV."

"You're probably right," she agrees. "Besides, we really don't want those kinds of movies coming into our living room."

"Those kind of movies?"

"Oh, you know, the kind with Ann-Margret in some slinky outfit or Bo Derek splashing around in a skimpy bathing suit or those other sexy things you can subscribe to if you have cable."

Suddenly it occurs to me that I may have been somewhat selfish on this cable TV question. After all, how would I feel if my children were deprived of some much-needed cultural experience just because I wouldn't cough up a few extra bucks a month?

On Saturday a man comes out and installs a little black box on top of our television and attaches it to some wires that disappear into a hole in the wall, and we have joined the cable generation.

Having grown up in a time when Lucy's pregnancy was a "condition" and the sight of Elvis from the waist down was a threat to Western civilization, I really am not prepared to join the cable generation, though. As I discover that night.

All day long the anticipation has been building as we prepare for our first evening of cable. Plans are made to stay up late to watch as many free movies as possible. The popcorn popper is cleaned out. Extra Kool-Aid is mixed.

"I don't want to ruin anybody's plans," I point out at the dinner table, "but if any of these movies are not suitable for kids, you aren't going to watch them. No sex, no violence, no profanity."

"What else is there?" asks the sixteen-year-old. "You've eliminated practically every movie for the past twenty years."

"Well, maybe there'll be a Mister Rogers film festival on."

"How about *History of the World, Part I?*" asks the thirteen-year-old. "That's on at ten."

"That doesn't sound too bad. I'm all for educational programs."

At ten o'clock, we get ready to watch the movie. It is a classic family scene. Two of the kids are lying on the floor in front of the TV. The eight-year-old is on my lap on the couch. The woman who promised to love, honor, and melt my butter is in the kitchen making popcorn. Any moment the doorbell will ring. It will be Ozzie looking for Harriet.

The movie begins. Immediately I sense that *History of the World, Part I* is not really an educational film. Perhaps it is because the star of the opening scene is Sid Caesar.

But the film is rather funny, so we sit there and munch popcorn and laugh through the Stone Age and past the Old Testament into the Roman Empire. We are in the middle of the decline when the big moment happens. A Roman soldier turns to another Roman soldier.

"Do you think the Empire will fall?" he asks.

"Bleep the Empire," says the other soldier.

An especially large kernel of popcorn stops halfway down

my throat. A dish hits the sink in the kitchen. Then there is silence. Our house has not been that quiet since the sixteen-year-old got her stereo fixed.

Finally, the woman who promised to love, honor, and punch my cuss button shouts from the kitchen, "What did he say?"

"I (choke, choke) don't know," I shout back. "I didn't hear him."

"I did," volunteers the thirteen-year-old, "he said . . ."

"NEVER MIND."

"I know how to spell that word," says the eight-year-old, the same eight-year-old who has trouble with cat, dog, and see Jane run. The spelling lesson is interrupted by the smack of the eight-year-old hitting the floor as I jump up from the couch to turn off the television.

"Well, OK, that's it," I announce, "time for you kids to go to bed."

"Why do we have to go to bed?" asks the thirteen-year-old. "It's not even eleven o'clock."

"Because Mom and Dad are tired."

Grumbling all the way, they head for their rooms.

It's not that I think seeing the rest of the movie would warp their minds or anything. On the other hand, if I wanted them to hear words like that, I would have let them hang around the last time I tried to replace a faucet washer.

Not only is that the year cable television invades our house, it also is the year of the outer space invasion. It is an attack that starts on the evening I tell my family that we are going out for dinner and all three boys climb into the backseat of the car wearing bags over their heads.

"What's with the bags?" I ask the woman who promised to love, honor, and keep me covered.

"They don't want anybody to be able to recognize them," she says.

"Why? Are they planning on holding up a liquor store?"

"Certainly not. It's just that they're embarrassed about being the only family in our plat without a video game."

"That can't be true. I'm sure there are plenty of homes in our neighborhood without video games. This bit about them being the only ones is just another of their exaggerations."

"Tell that to the eight-year-old's homeroom teacher. She's organizing a bake sale to raise money to buy him one."

I turn to the backseat.

"Is that true?" I ask.

The kid in the middle nods his bag.

We drive to the restaurant and eat. At separate tables. She sits with the three bags. At home that evening we continue the conversation.

"It's not that I have anything against video games," I explain. "It's just that I think their time would be better spent reading a book or riding their bikes or playing baseball. It has nothing to do with the fact that if we get a video game I'll have to use a machine gun to get to the television on Sunday afternoons to watch football. So I hope you understand and I hope they understand and I trust that this will be the end of the discussion. Now, I'm sort of tired and I think I'll be going up to bed. How about you?"

"I'll be along in a minute," she says. "As soon as I put on my bag."

The next day I ask the thirteen-year-old exactly what kind of video game he has in mind.

"Galaxian," he says. "It's an outer space game, and when you press the button a group of spaceships controlled by enemy aliens appears on the screen and showers you with bombs. It's excellent."

"Sounds fine with me," I say. "I'll go out and get one this weekend. How much does it cost?"

"Oh, about thirty dollars."

"Thirty bucks. You aren't serious. You expect me to shell out thirty dollars for some stupid game that showers you with illegal aliens?"

"Enemy aliens."

"Whatever. It's ridiculous."

"You're probably right, Dad. Just forget the whole thing. I imagine in three or four years I'll get over the effects of being the only kid in school who doesn't own a video outer space game."

"Quit being melodramatic. I never had an outer space game when I was a kid and I grew up all right."

"Mom says that when you were a kid they didn't know about outer space."

That weekend I drop in on a department store.

"Do you have a game called Galaxian?" I ask the clerk in the video department.

"I'm sorry," she says, "but we're all out. How about Odyssey?"

"Does it have a group of spaceships controlled by enemy aliens that showers you with bombs?"

"No. But it has flying saucers controlled by ill-tempered Martians that bombard you with laser blasts."

"Sorry. I don't think that's what he had in mind. I'll try another store."

"Do you have Galaxian?" I ask the man at the next store.

"Gee, I'm sorry, we just sold the last one. Could I interest you in a Gorok?"

"What does it have?"

"Space missiles controlled by bummed-out robots that strafe your command post with electronic beams."

"That's not quite what I'm looking for."

I try still another store.

"Galaxian?" I ask.

"Sold out three weeks ago. How about Aviary?"

"What does it have?"

"Large flocks of filthy birds that fly over your open convertible and bombard it with . . ."

"Skip it."

I spend the next two weeks going from store to store in

search of Galaxian. My efforts are unsuccessful, so I settle for some other games, and that weekend I spend an entire afternoon attaching a video game to the television with enough wires to confuse Thomas Edison. Eventually, I have it hooked up, and soon our house is filled with the happy sounds of electronic men being eaten alive by electronic alligators and electronic invaders being blown to electronic smithereens.

"This game is great, Dad," the thirteen-year-old says after a few hours. "Why don't you try it?"

He hands me a joystick and explains the purpose of the game, which is to guide a little electronic square through a series of rooms and mazes in search of a chalice.

In thirty seconds I have guided my electronic square into three walls, four blind alleys, and a dead-end.

"Better let me get you started, Dad," the thirteen-year-old says, grabbing the joystick. In ten seconds, the kid who can't drive a lawn mower once around the yard without destroying three thousand dollars' worth of privet hedge has guided the little electronic square out of the maze. He hands the joystick back to me.

I direct the electronic square through a large room. As I approach the doorway, a green figure appears on the screen. It looks like a duck. Before I can react, the thirteen-year-old grabs the joystick again and moves the electronic square in the other direction.

"Why did you run away from the green duck?" I ask.

"It's not a duck. It's a dragon. If he eats you, the game is over."

"Well, next time don't grab the joystick away from me. I'm not totally senile, you know."

I guide the electronic square through the room, past the doorway, and directly into the mouth of the green duck.

"Try again," he says, resetting the game.

After half an hour, he has reset the game seventeen times, I have guided the electronic square out of the maze seventeen times, and the green duck is so full he is racing around the electronic maze looking for Rolaids.

Still, the thirteen–year–old says that I am making progress and that someday when he and his friends go to a video arcade, they'll let me go along.

Of course, I'll have to wear a bag over my head.

# 6

## A CHIP OFF THE OLD JOCK

When it turns out that our firstborn son shows an interest in sports, I am a bit more enthusiastic about it than the woman who promised to love, honor, and polish my trophies.

Of course, she never had the sports career that I did. I'll never forget my sports career. It occurred in 1959. On a cool October day.

I was in eleventh grade then and I tried out for football, even though I weighed slightly under 140 pounds. Everybody on the football team weighed more than I did. Everybody on the cheerleading squad weighed more than I did. But what I lacked in size I made up for in cowardice. In no time at all I had worked my way to laststring halfback.

Still, I was on the team. When the season opened, I sat proudly on the bench, excitement surging through me as I saw, up close, my first real football game. So much excitement surged through me that I had to leave the bench to go back to the locker room. Three times.

As the game moved along, many of my teammates wished for victory. I wished for football pants with a zipper in front.

Not to mention a close game. The kind of game that would make it too risky for a coach to clear his bench and put in the subs.

I didn't get into that game. I didn't get into the next five games. But in the seventh game the coach sent me in as a deep man on the kickoff receiving team. Probably under the theory that anybody *that* small had to be fast.

Standing back there by the end zone, waiting for the kickoff, I knew beyond all doubt that if the other team kicked the ball in my direction and I caught it, I would never live to dance at the junior prom. I considered prayer. I considered lining up out of bounds. I considered a self-inflicted wound. But somehow I suspected that the coach wouldn't believe that I had torn my Achilles tendon while standing still.

Fortunately, the ball was kicked to a teammate and I didn't have to return it. Unfortunately, I did have to block. I ran upfield and looked for someone my size to hit. The only one I could find was a referee. So I picked out a middle-sized guy and threw a cross-body block at him, just like they taught us in practice. It was a beautiful block. I'll bet I didn't miss that guy by more than three or four yards.

As I trotted off the field, grass-stained and embarrassed, I heard a long, loud "boo" coming from the stands. That hurt. But it was nice to know that Mom had made it to the game.

But my career was not all highlights. And at the end of the year, when it became clear that Woody Hayes was not going to punch a hole in my front door to recruit me, I hung up my cleats.

But I always retained my love for the game, and I am pleased when our oldest son not only goes out for pee wee football but actually goes through an entire game without having to go back to the locker room.

"Sure," my wife says, "it's great for you. You get to sit up there in the stands with all the other fathers and trade lies about your touchdown runs. I'm the one who has to pick him up after practice. I'm the one who has to wash his football uniform. I'm the one who has to make brownies to sell at the concession stand. Besides, football is a dangerous game. What if he gets hurt?"

"He won't get hurt," I assure her. "I played football and I never got hurt."

"There's a big difference between you and him."

"What's that?"

"He'll probably make actual contact."

But I convince her that football isn't all that dangerous and that all those shots of pro football players on crutches are mainly insurance scams.

For two months she grumbles as she drives to practices, which always are ended ten or fifteen minutes late by coaches who stress that football is a game of split-second timing. For two months she scrubs his football pants, trying to get the grass stains out of his end zone. Before every game she takes brownies to sell at the concession stands. After every game she brings them home and feeds them to the dog.

Despite her fears, he survives his years of pee wee football without serious injury and advances to the junior-high team. Early in his eighth-grade season he breaks a bone in his right hand making a tackle. At the hospital they put his hand into a cast and tell us he'll have to wear it for six weeks.

"I told you football was a dangerous game," she says. "I'm not sure we should allow him ever to play again. It's just not worth the danger."

"You're overreacting," I say. "All he has is a broken bone in his hand. It's no big deal."

"No big deal? What about his schoolwork? That's his writing hand. His teachers won't be able to read his homework."

"His teachers never could read his homework," I point out. "If that kid ever becomes famous, he's going to have to type his autographs."

As it turns out, the broken hand proves to be more of a pain than either of us expected. Starting with that evening, when I remind him that it is the night that the garbage cans have to be carried from the garage out to the curb.

"Gosh, I'd really like to, Dad," he says, "but do you think that's a good idea? I mean, with this cast on my hand and all?"

"Oh, yeah, I didn't think about that. I guess you're right."

That night I carry the garbage cans out. All five of them. In the rain.

The next day when I come home from work there are some bags of water softener salt in front of the garage door.

"Don't forget to carry those bags of salt down to the utility room," I say to my football player son, who is sitting in the living room watching television.

"I can't lift those bags with this broken hand," he says. "Oh, and Dad, would you change the channel while you're here? It's really hard for me to turn the dial with this cast on."

"Oh. Sure."

I change the channel, go back to the garage, hoist the salt on my shoulder, and stagger down to the utility room.

An hour later, the woman who promised to love, honor, and fill my cart arrives home from the supermarket.

"Mom has groceries to carry in," I say.

Wordlessly, he holds up his cast. There is a little smile on his face. Wordlessly, I head back to the garage. There is no little smile on my face. I help her carry in the groceries. She carries the bag filled with three loaves of bread, a roll of toilet paper, and a bag of marshmallows. I get the bag with the ten cans of green beans, three quarts of applesauce, the ten-pound bag of potatoes, and the half gallon of melting ice cream.

I make it almost to the kitchen door before the jar of applesauce falls through the bottom of the bag. Onto my foot.

In the next six weeks, his broken hand prevents him from carrying groceries, lifting salt bags, toting garbage cans, making his bed, bringing in the mail, combing his hair, answering the phone, turning off the basement light, or watching his little brothers.

I, on the other hand, have a cold from carrying garbage cans in the rain, a pinched sciatic nerve from hoisting bags of salt, and a black toenail from falling applesauce jars.

I guess she was right, after all. Football is a dangerous game.

But, finally, the cast comes off his hand. The next day he announces that he is going out for wrestling.

It sounds like a great idea to me. When we both were much younger, he and I used to wrestle with each other nearly every evening. As soon as he had brushed his teeth and washed his face and put on his pajamas, he would run downstairs and we would roll around on the living room floor, giggling and tickling until his mother gave us the signal to quit. The signal always was the same: "I had him ready for bed and now you've gone and made him all sweaty."

I never did figure out why his being all sweaty made it tougher for him to go to bed. But I'd pin him to the floor one last time, tickle his soft little belly while he struggled helplessly, and then send him off to bed.

His soft little belly has become a hard little washboard now, and I think he'll make an excellent wrestler. His mother is not convinced.

"Why does he have to go out for wrestling?" she asks. "Why can't he just come home after school and waste time watching television like other kids?"

"It's only for two months," I point out. "Besides, in wrestling they don't get grass stains on their uniforms."

"But wrestling is more dangerous than football. What if he gets hurt again?"

"Wrestling probably is one of the least dangerous sports there is," I say.

"Don't give me that. I've seen what happens in wrestling. They spend an hour getting their heads bashed against the ring post and having some fat guy jump up and down on them, and then on their way to the dressing room a crazy lady jumps out of the crowd and starts smacking them with her purse and . . ."

"Good grief, that's not wrestling. That's rassling."

"What's the difference?"

"Plenty. Comparing rassling to wrestling is like comparing

MTV to music. Wrestling is a very scientific sport, with precise rules and strict officiating. There aren't any fat guys or ring posts. And the only crazy ladies are the wrestlers' mothers. Not only that, wrestling is a nice cheap sport. It's not like football, where we had to buy him cleats and a mouthguard and all that stuff."

So she relents and agrees that the thirteen-year-old may go out for wrestling, and the next day he comes home and says he needs twenty dollars for shoes.

"What's wrong with the shoes we bought for you last year?" I ask.

"These are for wrestling. We need special shoes."

I shell out twenty dollars for wrestling shoes, even though I do not quite understand why he needs special shoes for a sport in which the entire object is to roll around on the floor.

For the next three weeks he stays after school every day to get in shape for wrestling season. The practices may be building up his muscles, but they sure aren't helping his appetite much. I first begin to notice this at the dinner table one night when he helps himself to two pieces of spaghetti and a teaspoon of green beans.

"I thought spaghetti and green beans were your favorites," I say.

"They are," he says, "But I just had a snack before dinner."

"What was it?"

"A glass of water and a grape."

Immediately, my paternal instincts are aroused. This can't be the same kid who is accustomed to running home from school, sticking his head into the refrigerator, and grazing for two hours.

"What's going on?" I demand.

"Coach says I have to lose some weight."

"Lose some weight. You already look like Twiggy's under-nourished brother. I'll bet you don't weigh more than 110 pounds."

"One hundred three," he says. "But I've got to get down to 100. Coach says I'd do better in a lower weight class."

It occurs to me that if he really wants to lose three pounds in a hurry, he could get a haircut, but I don't say that and everything is calm until a few days later when I arrive home to find his mother looking rather upset.

"What's the matter?" I ask.

"It's the thirteen-year-old," she says. "Every day when he gets home all he wants to do is practice wrestling holds."

"So?"

"He's practicing them on us. Already today he's pinned each of his little brothers three times and won a referee's decision from his sister. He's driving us crazy with this wrestling stuff."

"You're exaggerating."

"You think so? Just before you walked in the door he was trying to get a half-nelson on the dog."

After dinner I mention to the thirteen-year-old that maybe he'd better ease off on the wrestling homework.

"Coach says we should practice as much as possible," he replies. "Coach says that it would be really good to practice with your father, even though he's probably fat and out of shape. How about it? Want to wrestle?"

I make a mental note to vote against the next school levy that would give Coach a raise and follow the thirteen-year-old into the family room. There I assume the classic wrestling position: hands in front, feet spread, weight balanced on the balls of the feet, stomach sucked in.

"Ready?" he asks.

"Ready."

The next thing I know my legs are flying out from under me and I'm flat on my back on the family room floor. Before I have a chance to react, my shoulders are being pressed against the shag carpet. I have been pinned by a 100-pound thirteen-year-old.

But even worse is that, while I struggle helplessly, he begins to tickle my soft little belly.

For two months we drive him to wrestling practices, which are run by guys who can't tell time any better than football coaches. For two months his mother prepares diet dinners so he can lose two pounds in the next fifteen minutes and make weight. For two months we go to wrestling meets together, even though she doesn't know a referee's position from a missionary position.

Finally the season ends, we go to the wrestling banquet, and the thirteen-year-old turns in his suit.

The next day he announces that he is joining the weight-lifting program.

"Weight lifting," exclaims the woman who promised to love, honor, and press my bench. "Is this the same kid who says carrying out the garbage will give him a hernia?"

"It's only for two months," I point out. "Besides, weight lifting is good conditioning."

For two months we drive him to weight-lifting sessions, which are run by guys whose watches have been crushed by barbells. For two months she goes to the grocery store every hour on the hour to keep food in the house so the kid can "bulk up." For two months she tries not to notice when she sees him military-pressing her washing machine.

Finally weight lifting ends and the thirteen-year-old turns in his biceps.

"Thank God," says his mother, "this sports stuff is all over for the year. I looked at the calendar and I have six whole months before football practice starts again."

"Yep," I say.

I don't have the heart to tell her about swimming season.

To tell the truth, I wasn't even prepared for swimming season myself. Where I grew up, kids never got wet on purpose. But when the thirteen-year-old says that he'd like to join a swim team during the summer, I'm all for it.

"Idle hands are the Devil's instruments," I point out to the woman who promised to love, honor, and minimize my maxims. "A healthy teenager needs athletics to help him use up all that excess energy."

"Are we talking about the same teenager?" she demands. "The one who needs CPR to get his heart going long enough to go out and check the mail?"

"Well, maybe he's not a compulsive worker around the house," I concede. "But I guarantee that being active is good for him."

Each morning that summer, the thirteen-year-old goes off to swim practice. Each afternoon he comes home reeking of chlorine. Each weekend he goes off with the team for a swim meet. In less than a month we notice a definite change in him. All the other teenagers in the neighborhood are developing pimples. He's growing gills.

But he enjoys moderate success as a freestyler, and I am not really surprised when I get a call from him one afternoon telling me that he has qualified for the regional finals.

"That's terrific, son," I say. "When are they?"

"Today at 5:30. I'll need a ride. It's sixty miles."

"It's 4:30 already and I'm right in the middle of work. Can't your mother take you?"

"I asked her, but she said that you'd be glad to do it. She said that being active would be good for you. Oh, and she also said something about idle hands being the Devil's instruments. What's that supposed to mean?"

"It means that I'll pick you up in fifteen minutes."

I leave work, pick him up, and we race to the regional meet. When we arrive, the pool is filled with swimmers taking practice laps. Along one side of the pool, three rows of hard steel bleachers are filled with parents wearing stop watches around their necks. I squeeze into a front-row seat right near the starting blocks.

Just as I sit down, a swimmer in lane one takes a practice dive and enough water to sink Maui splashes into my lap. Seconds later another swimmer hits the water and another tidal wave rolls over me. Swimmer after swimmer sends wave after wave over me. After ten minutes I am in danger of becoming the first person ever to drown at a swimming meet while sitting in the stands.

Finally, practice is over and the teams gather around their coaches for last-minute instructions. I turn to the parent sitting next to me.

"Excuse me, but do you have any idea how long this meet will take? I don't want to miss dinner."

"This your first meet?" he asks.

"As a matter of fact, it is. How did you know?"

"Swim parents who have been around for a while don't worry about missing dinner. They worry about missing presidential terms."

He nudges the parent next to him.

"This guy's worried about missing dinner," he snickers.

"What's dinner?" the other parent asks.

"Remember the AAU meet?" the guy next to me asks him.

"That the one that was in June?"

"And July. Of course, it wasn't a full meet. The only event they finished was the 5,000-meter dog paddle. My favorite was the '79 sectionals."

"They finish that already?"

"The last I heard, they were in the twelfth heat of the 10,000-meter Australian crawl."

"My kid did 0:53.1 in that."

"Not bad. My oldest kid had an 0:49.2 in the tryouts for the '76 Olympics."

"Terrific. Did he make the team?"

"He would have, but the tryouts lasted until 1978."

They both turn to me.

"What's your kid's best time?"

"I'm not sure. I think I heard him say something about breaking ten minutes. Is that a good time?"

"Not unless he's swimming the English Channel," one of them says, turning his attention back to his stopwatch.

It's obvious that I have a lot to learn as a swim-team parent. Not the least of which is how a kid who can swim 100 meters in less than a minute can take an hour and a half to shower afterward. But it looks as if I'm going to have plenty of time to figure it out.

But swimming season finally does gurgle to an end. Then we are back at another football season. It is the one that will forever be known in our family as the year of the fly pattern.

It is the final game of the season, the annual rivalry with the junior high across town. We get there early so I can get a good place to stand on the top row of the bleachers. Standing on the top row of the bleachers is sort of a tradition. The mothers all sit together in a middle row and complain about how hard it is to get football socks clean. The fathers all stand on the top row and lie to each other about how much they don't care if their kid makes first string and that all that counts is that they're building character and learning sportsmanship.

In the first quarter, our team gets the ball and moves smartly down the field all the way to the three-yard line. But on second down, the nose guard from the crosstown rival breaks through and smears our quarterback.

"Some dummy missed his block," the father standing next to me gripes.

A woman two rows in front of us turns around.

"Watch it, buster," she snaps, "that's my dummy you're talking about."

Eventually, our team loses the ball. What's worse, it's getting colder. The wind is whistling across the field. Our defense runs out to try to stop the crosstown rivals. The wind is whistling through the stands. Our defense gets the ball back. The wind is whistling down my pants leg.

A flush of embarrassment starts at the back of my neck and slinks around to my cheeks. It's been quite some time since I've forgotten to zip up. Several weeks, at least.

Casually, my eyes never leaving the action down on the field, I take one hand out of my pocket and let it sort of meander down to where the little tab of the zipper is. But the little tab, I discover, is not down at the bottom. It is still up at the top. I didn't forget, after all. The zipper is broken.

I am happy to discover that I did not forget. But my joy lasts only until I realize that I am standing there with a permanently open fly and a jacket that reaches only to my waist. In front of about 150 people. Half of whom are teenagers. And the other half of whom are officers in the PTA.

I have three options.

I can sit down, which means I will miss the rest of the game, because the guy in front of me is Wilt Chamberlain's big brother.

I can race through the stands, tell the guy at the gate I am going home to change my pants, ignore his expression, drive home, find some slacks with an unbroken zipper, put them on, drive back, and race to my spot in the bleachers. Which also means I will miss the rest of the game.

Or I can stand there and fake it.

I put my hands back into my pockets, push the teeth of the zipper back together as best I can and sort of crouch over. As long as I can keep my hands in my pockets, I might be all right.

In the second quarter, our team scores. I am the only father on the top row who does not applaud. But I make it to halftime with no further problems, and, after the final play of the second quarter, I walk down the steps in search of the woman who promised to love, honor, and keep me covered. I spot her sitting with a group of other mothers. She sees me walking toward her, crouched over, with my hands in my pockets.

"YOU SHOULDN'T COME TO THESE GAMES IF YOU'RE GOING TO GET AN UPSET STOMACH OVER THEM," she shouts. She has to shout, because the band has started playing the school fight song.

"MY STOMACH'S NOT UPSET," I shout back. "MY ZIPPER'S BROKEN."

"WHAT?"

"I SAID, I'M NOT UPSET . . . "

The band suddenly finishes playing the school fight song.

" . . . MY ZIPPER'S BROKEN."

Dozens of parents stop in mid-conversation to stare at me. I feel like I'm in the middle of an E.F. Hutton commercial. There's nothing I can do but stand there and smile. I'm certainly not going to wave.

The woman who promised to love, honor, and keep me covered forages around in her purse and finally comes up with a safety pin.

"Here," she says, "close it up with this."

"You know I'm all thumbs with safety pins. How's it going to look if I stand here for twenty minutes fumbling with my zipper?"

"Well, I suppose I could do it for you," she says. "But my hands are pretty cold. I can't guarantee I'll be able to get the pin exactly where I'm aiming."

"I'll do it myself."

Eventually I get the zipper safety-pinned back together. With the hole in my defense covered, I rejoin the other fathers on the top row. Our team comes out in the second half, scores two more touchdowns, and defeats the crosstown rival.

"The coach must have really made some adjustments at halftime," the father next to me says when the final whistle blows. "That's probably what got them going in the second half."

Perhaps. But I prefer to think they won this one for the zipper.

It is a memorable game for me. But it is, it turns out, even more significant for our oldest son.

He was nine years old when he started playing football, and he really wasn't very good at it back then. His football pants flapped loosely on skinny legs and his shoulder pads were so big that he couldn't lift his arms high enough to catch a pass, and he really wasn't big enough for the helmet they gave him. Or for the plastic cup they made him wear.

In blocking drills that first year he ran into his opponent sideways like a movie hero knocking down a door, and in tackling practice he ducked his head just before the ball carrier got to him, and everybody liked to run against him because he made them all look like O.J. Simpson. Even on a team that lost all its games and went an entire season without scoring, he was not very good.

But he stayed with it and did what he could with what he had because he knew his father loved football and would be very proud of him if he did.

When he was ten years old he got a little better and the coach discovered that he could run pretty fast once he finally got used to carrying all that equipment. They made him a running back and, in the middle of the season, he scored his first touchdown.

That was a big moment for him, because his mother and his Aunt Sue and his Uncle Charlie were up in the stands. And, of course, so was his father, who was at all the games and almost every practice and never tired of going out into the backyard after dinner to pass a few.

When he was eleven years old most of the kids on the football team had spent the summer growing a lot, and just about every one of them was bigger than he was. Just before the season started, the coach told him that he was being dropped to the "B" team. The hurt still was in his eyes when his father showed up for practice that afternoon.

But that turned out to be the best thing that ever happened to him. Because on the "B" team he was a star, the quarterback on offense, the safety on defense. He had a season of which dreams are made. He passed or ran for nineteen touchdowns, and no team scored against them until the final game of the season.

His team was behind in that game until the final minute, and on fourth down they called his number and he ran wide on a sweep for a first down, with his father standing on the sidelines screaming for him to go out of bounds and stop the clock. But he cut upfield instead and twisted and struggled and finally broke free and went all the way for the touchdown that won the game and made the season perfect.

After the game the whole team went out for pizza and all the cheerleaders wanted to sit with him, and when somebody started a cheer, the loudest was saved for him. His father sat at a table with the coaches, and he knew that his father was very, very proud.

The next week the editor of the local paper wrote a whole column about the team, and most of it was about him. His father cut out the column and put it in his desk with his other treasures. Not long after that, his father met the head coach of the high school varsity and the coach said that he had read the column and was looking forward to having him on the team in a few years. His father's chest stayed puffed out for two weeks.

When he was twelve he was a starter on the seventh-grade team as a cornerback, and he shared the quarterback job with a kid who was half a foot taller and a couple of years older. There was no way he could match what he had done the year before, but he worked hard and tried his best. He knew that his father was up there in the stands, sitting with all the other fathers, each of them cheering loudly for the team, but each of them cheering even louder inside for his son to do better than all the other sons.

When he was thirteen he broke his hand trying to tackle a runner who was thirty pounds heavier than he was. For the rest of the season he couldn't do much more than sit around and watch football on television with his father. They agreed that he probably would never be a pro football player but that he was sure to be a starter in high school and maybe he would get at least a partial scholarship to a small school somewhere.

When he was fourteen he had to fight for his job as a starter, because by now he was just about the smallest kid on the team and when there was a huddle, his was the helmet that you couldn't see.

When he was fifteen he went to all the preseason weight-lifting sessions and he endured the conditioning program and he went to the first two weeks of practice. And one afternoon he came home and told his mother that he was sick of football and that he was quitting the team. His mother was glad.

That evening he missed dinner and when he came home his father was in the living room, reading the paper.

"Did Mom tell you?" he asked.

"Yes, she told me."

"You don't seem very mad about it. I thought you'd be mad."

"I'm not mad. If you don't want to play football anymore, that's your decision.

"OK. I'm glad you're not mad."

He walked away then and left his father sitting there in the living room, alone with his newspaper and his dreams. He was fifteen. It was time for him to dream his own dreams.

# 7

## MR. BADWRENCH

When I bought my MG Midget, everybody told me that I was making a mistake. MG Midgets are stupid little cars, they said. MG Midgets never start in the winter, they said. You'll be sorry, they said.

My friends told me I'd be sorry. My neighbors told me I'd be sorry. People who had refused to talk to me in years called up to tell me I'd be sorry. None of that really bothered me, although I do have to admit that I was a little concerned when the MG Midget salesman told me I'd be sorry.

But I bought the car anyway, and, as it turned out, all those people were wrong. I didn't have any trouble starting my MG Midget in the winter. I had trouble starting my MG Midget in the summer. Each time the temperature got over eighty degrees, the car refused to start. Not only did I have a stupid little car, I had a confused stupid little car.

But after a few years of confusion, I finally get things straightened out. After a few years of confusion, it won't run in the winter, either.

The first time it happens is on a winter day when the temperature is in the teens and the car has been parked at work for eight hours. When I try to start it, the engine makes a lot of grinding noises, but fails to turn over. I try again. More grinding noises. I try a third time. This time the grinding noises are quieter and deeper in tone. I keep trying. When the engine starts to sound like Jerome Hines with a cold, I am convinced that it will not start.

There is only one logical thing left to do. I get out of the car and kick the fender. That doesn't get the car started, but it makes me feel a lot better. Except for my right foot, which is radiating pain into my calf. Just as the pain reaches my knee, a co-worker comes up behind me. It is obvious that he has seen me kick my car.

"Having trouble getting it started?" he asks.

"No, I'm practicing for a tryout as a placekicker with the Cincinnati Bengals. The first guy who can put a sports car through the uprights from thirty-five yards out gets the job."

"How about if I give you a jump from my battery?"

"Thanks."

"I'll get my car into position and you get out your jumper cables."

"Jumper cables?"

"Don't tell my you drive an MG Midget in the winter without jumper cables."

I hang my head in embarrassment.

"Well, never mind," he says. "I'll give you a push to get you started."

He maneuvers his Pontiac into position behind my MG.

"How does it line up?" he calls from his car.

"Not real great," I call back.

"Define 'not real great.' "

"Well, your bumper is even with my rear window."

Despite this inconvenience, we manage to get the car started, and I drive it home and park it in my warm garage. The next morning it will not start. At this point, I have three options. I can take the new station wagon that belongs to the woman who promised to love, honor, and clean my plugs. I can take the old Buick that belongs to the sixteen-year-old. I can wait for spring.

Of the three, taking the new station wagon is the least desirable. Every time I take her car, she gets upset.

"If I don't have a car, I'm stuck in the house all day," she points out.

"So? Why do you need to go out?"

"Something important might come up that I'll need the car for."

"Like what?"

"Like, maybe there'll be a one-day-only sale at J.C. Penney's. Without a car I wouldn't be able to get there."

"If J.C. Penney's has a sale and you don't show up, they'll send a limousine for you. And J.C. himself will be driving it."

Rather than go through all that hassle, I take the sixteen-year-old's aged Buick. Although it's twelve years old, it's in pretty good shape, except that it doesn't have a radio. Then again, it has about a million holes in the muffler, so it really doesn't matter. I start the car. It roars to life with enough noise to register on the Richter scale. I check the gas gauge. It is about half full. It's a five-mile drive to work. It'll be close.

For the next four days I drive to work in a car that's louder than Jerry Lewis and thirstier than Dean Martin. On my way home from work the fifth day, I hear a noise that is even louder than the muffler. A few miles later, steam begins to surge out of the front end of the car. Between the noise from the muffler and the steam from the engine, it is like driving Mount St. Helens.

The problem, I discover when I get home, is that there is a hole in the radiator hose.

So now I have an old car in the driveway with a hole in the radiator hose. A small car in the repair shop with an allergy to winter and summer. A new car in the garage with the keys hidden where I never will find them.

In spite of it all, I still have not become totally disenchanted with my MG Midget. With all of its problems, it's still a fun car to drive. But only during the second week in May.

That's the time of year that MG Midgets are made for. Because late spring is the convertible owner's revenge.

Through the snows of winter, convertible owners drive with one hand on the wheel and the other chipping ice off of the heater. Through the rains of early spring, convertible owners drive with one hand on the wheel and the other on the sump pump.

But in late spring, convertible owners drive with the wind in their hair and the sun in their faces, alive and carefree, with nothing more serious to worry about than sudden thunderstorms and nasty birds.

So when the following May arrives, I put the top down, turn on the engine, and take it for a ride. To the mechanic's.

"I think there's something wrong with it," I tell him.

"Can you describe the problem?"

"Well, for one thing, there's smoke coming out of the tail pipe."

"Smoke is supposed to come out of the tail pipe."

"When the engine's off?"

"Sounds like a valve job. I'll call you when it's ready."

Not more than a month later, he calls me. As we drive it home, the woman who promised to love, honor, and clean my dipstick says she notices a strong smell inside the car."

"That's probably because I just filled it with gas," I point out.

"Where did you put it, in the glove compartment?"

Half a mile later, the car stops.

"Leaky hose," the mechanic says when I get it back to the garage. "I'll call you when it's ready."

Ten days later he calls me. I drive it home. By now it is early June. Perfect top-down weather. I smile with pity at the stodgy drivers I pass in their cooped-up little cars. Just as I am smiling with pity at a stodgy driver in his cooped-up little VW, my transmission falls out.

"I'll call you when it's ready," says the mechanic when the tow truck operator has driven away.

Two weeks later he calls me. I drive it home. It is in perfect shape now but full of greasy fingerprints. I park it on the edge of my lawn and wash it until it sparkles. When it is dry, I put the top down. Another perfect day for a drive. I start the car, push in the clutch, and try to shift into first. The clutch stays on the floor. The car stays in neutral. I call the mechanic.

"Sounds like a leaky seal," he says. "I'll come out in a few days and look at it."

"What do I do with it in the meantime? I can't leave it sitting on the edge of my lawn."

"Kick-start it," he suggests. "Turn off the key, slip it into second, then turn on the key. You can drive it in second long enough to get it to your garage."

I follow his instructions. When I turn the key, the car jerks to life and lurches forward. Since I can't back it up, the easiest way to get it to the garage is by making a U-turn through my front lawn. I drive forward to the middle of the yard. Which is where the car stalls. I try to kick-start it again. This time the car lurches forward six inches but does not start. I try again. Six more inches. No more starts. It is roughly seventy feet from where the car is to where the garage is. Or 140 more lurches.

As I sit there in my car, with the top down, in the middle of my lawn, every person I have ever met drives past, slows down, and delivers an hysterically funny comment.

"Hey, D.L., must have been a pretty good party last night. You really missed the garage."

"Yeah. Ha, ha, ha."

"Hey, D.L., I love your new lawn ornament."

"Yeah."

"Hey, D.L., is that the latest in patio furn—"

"Shut up."

Eventually I get the car pushed into the garage. The way things are going, it will be November before this car is running right. But look for me on the road, then. I'll be the one with the top down.

As embarrassing as it is to have your car break down in the middle of your front yard, it is not the most embarrassing place in the world. The most embarrassing place in the world is in front of the biggest X-rated movie theater in town. Which is where it breaks down a few months later.

I am on my way to work when it happens. One moment I am cruising along, listening to the stereo sounds of my springs squeaking. The next moment I am at a red light with my engine revving and something in my clutch assembly snapped like a broken G-string.

When the light changes I manage to coast toward the nearest parking lot and get the front end of the car into the driveway before it comes to a halt. My front bumper is in the parking lot of a theater where this week's XXX-rated attractions are *Body Love, Oriental Babysitters*, and *Happy Hitchhiking Housewives.* My rear bumper is sticking out into a street where car horns are blowing and tempers are about to.

I have no choice. I get out of the car, walk to the rear bumper, and begin to shove. Not only will people see me going into the parking lot of the dirty movie theater, they will see me pushing my car to get there.

When the car is in the lot, I look around for a phone so that I can call the woman who promised to love, honor, and iron my raincoat. There is no phone anywhere in sight. The nearest one probably is in the lobby of the theater. I walk to the entrance and pause. This is all very embarrassing. I have never been in an adult movie theater before. During the daytime.

A lady behind the counter is reading a book when I walk in. She looks up.

"That'll be six bucks," she says.

"I want to call my wife," I say.

"We don't give family discounts here," she says.

"You don't understand. My car is broken down and I need her to pick me up."

She shrugs and points to a pay phone. I dial my number. While I wait for her to answer, I glance around the lobby. Next to the popcorn machine is a video recorder showing a sample of the X-rated movie cassettes on sale here. Having nothing better to do, I watch it while the phone rings. The movie is a simple yet effective film about a man, a woman, and forty-seven minutes of moaning. After fifty or sixty rings, I conclude that no one is home at my house. I call my mechanic.

"Gee, I'd like to help you," he says. "But I'm here all alone today."

"Well, what am I supposed to do, sit around in the lobby of this X-rated theater all day and watch a bunch of movies about people in heat who . . ."

"I'll be right over."

I go back outside to the parking lot and wait for the mechanic to show up. As I stand there, in front of an adult theater, leaning against a car with my initials on the license plates, everyone I ever have met just happens to drive by at fifteen miles an hour. I could be helping old ladies across the street and no one I knew ever would see me. I could stand in front of the Vatican for a year and never be recognized. But stand in front of a dirty movie house for ten seconds and it starts to look like "This Is Your Life."

Eventually, the mechanic arrives and pokes around under the car for a while.

"Doesn't look like anything too serious," he says. "I can probably fix it right here. But I'm going to have to get something to eat first. I didn't have time for lunch."

"I don't think there are any restaurants around here," I say.

"I'll just go in and get some popcorn."

He disappears into the lobby of the X-rated theater. Less than forty-five minutes later he returns.

"What took so long?" I ask.

"I was getting extra butter."

Two hours and nine boxes of popcorn later, he has the car fixed.

"Thanks very much for coming out," I tell him as he starts to drive away.

"My pleasure," he says. "See you next week."

A week later the car is back in the shop.

"You know," he says, "you could save yourself a lot of aggravation if you'd learn how to do some of these repairs yourself."

"I could save myself a lot of aggravation if I just parked it on top of a hill with the emergency brake off."

"No, really, it's not all that difficult to find your way around an engine."

"Are you kidding? It took me two years to find out how to operate the windshield wipers on this thing. The first time I had a flat tire I had to call the Auto Club to open my trunk."

"Well, maybe I can give you a few tips. Why did you bring it in this time?"

"It's not operating at peak efficiency."

"What do you mean, exactly?"

"It hasn't started in six days."

"Probably the points. Have you checked them lately?"

"No, but I'm sure they're still there. I always park it in the garage at night and nobody . . ."

"I meant, did you check to see if they're stuck? Here, let me show you."

He pops open the hood, reaches into the engine, flicks two clips that hold the distributor cap in place, reaches in with a screwdriver, and wiggles it around for a few seconds.

"Start it up," he says.

I turn the key in the ignition. Instantly there is a noise from underneath the hood.

"What's that noise?" I shout.

"It's your engine running."

"I thought it sounded familiar."

As I drive the car home, it occurs to me that it was not real

smart of him to show me how to fix the car myself. If I can fix it,
I won't need his services as often. All I can figure is that my
visits are putting him in a higher tax bracket.

A few days later the car doesn't start. But this time I am
prepared. Mentally I review the procedure he showed me. Pop
open the hood, flick the clips, wiggle with a screwdriver, and
start the car. I set to work. In less than twenty minutes I have
popped open the hood.

Inside the engine I locate the distributor cap, which is
conveniently situated beneath eight miles of wires. There is just
enough room between the wires for me to slide my forefinger
down to the clips. I push as hard as I can on one of the clips. I
withdraw my forefinger. I go inside, wash off the blood, put on a
bandage, and return to the garage.

This time I use a screwdriver to push down on the clip. The
clip pops off. The second clip comes off even more easily. I take
off the distributor cap, reach in with the screwdriver, and
separate the points. There is nothing to it, and I have just saved
myself a sizeable repair bill. Elated, I reach in to replace the
distributor cap. An hour later I still am reaching in to replace
the distributor cap. Perhaps, I reason, the distributor cap is not
firmly in place. I tap the top of it gently with the handle of the
screwdriver. No help. I tap it less gently. Still no help. I switch
from a screwdriver to a hammer. I rap the distributor cap
smartly with the hammer. I am rewarded by the sound of a sharp
snap as the distributor cap cracks.

Defeated, I throw the hammer back into the tool box and
reach for the hood to slam it down. The hood does not slam
down. The hood does not even move. I go into the house. I have
a bandage on my thumb, a crack in my distributor cap, a hood
that won't close, a car that won't start, and a sneaking suspicion
that the repair bill this time will be twice as big as it would have
been if I hadn't tried to fix it myself.

Not to mention a real smart mechanic.

As cars go, that MG Midget seldom did. In six years, it
turned just 42,000 miles on the odometer. And 20,000 of

those came when it was attached to the back of a tow truck. Which is not to suggest that it was a totally worthless car. After all, it provided the money to send three kids to college. Unfortunately, they were my mechanic's kids.

But I always figured that when I finally had to get rid of it, it would be for some fairly significant reason. Like because the engine exploded. The transmission dropped out. The chassis dropped out. All on the same day. I never guessed that it would be because of a grease spot. But then, I forgot about the woman who promised to love, honor, and drain my crankcase.

To be fair, she was pretty patient during the whole terrible ordeal. On the day I bought the car, she actually rode in it with me when we went out to dinner that night. Of course, she took the bus home from the restaurant. But only because there wasn't room enough for both of us in the tow truck.

But she kept her temper through brake jobs and broken muffler clamps. In spite of radiators that blew and horns that didn't. When the interior carpeting wore out in the first year, she never said a thing. Although that may have been because the interior lights burned out in the first month. She never complained about the noisy muffler. At least, I never heard her.

But she loses her cool when she sees the grease spot.

In terms of size, the grease spot is invisible to the human eye. But she sees it five seconds after it appears on the living room carpet. Of course, she is the kind of housekeeper who could find filth inside an oxygen tent.

"Look at this terrible grease spot," she shrieks, pointing to the floor.

"What grease spot?" I ask, bending over to look.

"Right here," she says, pulling me down to my hands and knees.

"I still don't see it."

"Look closer."

"What do you mean, look closer? I've already got rug burns on my forehead."

"It's right here under my fingernail."

At last I see it. It is either a very small grease spot or a very large microbe.

"It's not exactly the Santa Monica oil spill," I point out.

"It looks awful. What will people think?"

"When's the last time people crawled through our living room on their hands and knees?"

"The night you had your office party here. Anyway, it ruins the looks of the whole house, and it's all the fault of that stupid little car of yours."

"Now wait a minute. How did you arrive at that conclusion?"

"It's obvious. Some grease probably dripped down your clutch pedal and you got it on your left foot and tracked it into the living room and now the whole place looks like Gasoline Alley."

"That's really ridiculous. I've seen exposes in the *National Enquirer* that were based on better evidence than that. But, if it will make you happy, I'll go out and check."

I walk out into the garage, open my car door, start to get in, and nearly break my kneecap when my left foot slips on the puddle of black grease that has collected under my clutch pedal.

"Well?" she demands, when I return to the house.

"OK, you were right. But I'm sure it's something that's easily corrected. It's probably just some minor malfunction. Like a broken driveshaft or something."

"I'll never understand what possessed you to buy such a stupid little car," she snaps. "There's not one good thing about that car."

"Oh no? How about the great mileage it gets? That car can go a month on one tank of gas."

"Of course it can. Why shouldn't it? It spends five days out of every week at the repair shop."

"You just don't understand about sports cars. They're temperamental."

"The Boston Strangler was temperamental. That car is psychotic. Every time I go to the post office I expect to see its picture hanging on the wall. I'm telling you, you're going to have to make a choice. It's either me or that car. There's not room enough in this family for both of us."

It's a tough decision. That car has a pretty good radio in it. Not to mention a new muffler. On the other hand, she has less rust on her.

"OK," I say finally, "we'll go look for a new car tomorrow."

The next day I decide to take the whole family out to look for a new car. The kids probably will enjoy it. I loved to visit car showrooms with my parents when I was a kid. We never could afford to buy anything, but it was exciting to leaf through the glossy brochures and fun to look at the shiny paint jobs and inhale the special aroma that the interiors of new cars always have. Then I would go home and dream of some day being rich enough to own a new car.

"I think it will be a great experience for the kids," I point out to the woman who promised to love, honor, and kick my tires.

"Well, if nothing else, when you walk into a showroom with an eight-year-old whose hobby is slamming car doors, you get pretty fast attention from the salesmen," she says.

We drive to a nearby car dealer. Before the eight-year-old can get his first door open, a salesman wearing a "Buy American" pin in his lapel and a Seiko on his wrist is in my face.

"May I help you?"

"We really don't have anything special in mind," I tell him. "We just want to get an idea of what's available."

"Perhaps if you could tell me what price range you're thinking of, I can show you what we have."

I tell him what price range I'm thinking of. He tells me that he didn't realize it was Soap Box Derby time already.

"You mean what I want to spend isn't enough for a good car?" I demand.

"What you want to spend is not enough for a good down payment," he says.

I drag the eleven-year-old out from behind the wheel of a $10,000 economy car and head for another dealer.

"Don't touch anything," I instruct the kids as we walk into the showroom. "Dent a bumper in one of these places and we'll be in debt for the rest of our lives."

A salesman approaches us.

"I'm looking for something not too expensive," I tell him. "You know, something that the average working man can afford."

He leads me to a rather drab-looking car with black tires and a stick shift. I glance at the sticker on the rear window. His idea of an average working man apparently is Reggie Jackson.

"All right," I say, "let's stop fooling around. I want to see the cheapest car in the place. One of those $5,000 jobs you see in the TV commercials."

"Follow me," he says.

"We follow him out the back door of the showroom. Through the service area. Down an alley. Into an unheated garage. He flips on a light switch. Standing in the corner is the $5,000 car I have seen on television. It looks much homelier in person. And much smaller. Not only do I have a sports car at home that is bigger than this, I have a sports coat at home that is bigger.

"I don't think you'd be comfortable in a car that size," whispers the woman who promised to love, honor, and stay out of my space.

"I don't think Tattoo would be comfortable in a car that size."

"Actually, through clever engineering, they've managed to make it very roomy inside," the salesman says. "See for yourself."

I wedge my head inside the car. He's right. The clever engineers have taken advantage of every inch. By leaving out the radio, glove compartment, arm rests, carpet, cigarette lighter, and rear seat.

"I've ridden in canoes with more equipment in them than this," I mention.

"Well, of course it has a full line of options. But that will run the price up a little." He whips out a calculator and computes the cost of fully equipping the car. For under $8,000 I can have a car complete with AM–FM radio, air conditioning, automatic transmission, cigarette lighter, and enough leg room for me and the dwarf of my choice. I thank him and we leave.

For the next three months our evenings are filled with showroom visits, test drives, and salesmen with firm handshakes and smiles sincere enough to embarrass Jimmy Carter. Eventually, I have narrowed it down to two choices. Either I will get a sensible, no-frills, *Consumer Reports*-approved subcompact that gets four months to the gallon, or I will get the car that I want.

The car I want comes with a V–8 engine, a five-speed gearshift, AM–FM stereo, convertible top, and a lifetime guarantee that I will never hear the end of it from the woman who promised to love, honor, and share my garage.

"How could you even consider throwing our money away on a car like that?" she snaps as we stand in the showroom looking at it. "And stop drooling."

"What's wrong with that car?" I ask, wiping my chin. "Just look at how beautiful it is. Look at that engine. Look at those lines. Look at that beautiful red paint job."

"Yeah. All that's missing is a siren and a dalmation."

"Well, maybe it is a little bright," I concede. "But at least it would be easy to see during a fog."

"It would be easy to see during an eclipse," she says. "I just can't believe you'd even have the nerve to be seen driving down the street in anything that gaudy."

"What are you saying, that I'd feel self-conscious in that car?"

"There are pimps who would feel self-conscious in that car."

Our conversation is interrupted by a salesman who approaches us with a sincere smile and crushes my knuckles.

"Impressive car, isn't it folks?" he says.

"Beautiful," I say.

"Just what every forty-year-old man needs for cruising McDonald's parking lot," she says.

"Did you notice the color-keyed Rally wheels?" the salesman says.

"Beautiful," I say.

"What kind of mileage does it get?" she says.

"Uh, let me show you the electric rear-window defogger," the salesman says.

"Beautiful," I say.

"Mileage," she says.

"Well, of course, mileage figures can be deceptive," he says. "A lot depends upon your driving habits."

"In other words," she says, "if we buy this car, Standard Oil stock goes up twelve points."

"Did I mention that it comes with a digital quartz clock?" the salesman says. "Plus, it has reclining bucket seats. A full-grown man could sleep in those seats."

"If he buys this car, he's going to have to," she says. "Besides, the sub-compact cars we were looking at have reclining bucket seats, a digital quartz clock, a rear-window defogger, color-keyed Rally wheels, and they get forty-eight miles to the gallon."

"I'm sure they're very nice cars," the salesman says. "Of course, if you have a family, you might find it a little bit cramped. This car is big enough so that your husband can stop on his way home from work and pick up an entire week's worth of groceries."

"I never thought of that," she admits.

"Then there's that nice big backseat, which is roomy enough for him to take all the kids to Little League practice. And, on those days when you're too busy to . . ."

I grab her arm and drag her out of the showroom. For the

life of me, I can't imagine why she'd even consider such a gaudy car.

Finally, we find a car that we agree on. We select the color we want, pick the options we need, and negotiate the price. The only thing that remains is to find out what kind of a deal I can get on my old car.

"What kind of a car is it?" the salesman asks.

"An MG Midget," I tell him. "Are you familiar with them?"

"Only by their nickname."

"Nickname?"

"The English Edsel. Tell me, what kind of condition would you say it's in?"

"Oh, it's about in average shape for a Midget."

"That bad, huh? Well, if I can find a mechanic who doesn't have any dependents, I'll have him take it for a test drive. Are the jumper cables in it?"

"Front seat."

Half an hour later, the mechanic returns from the test drive. He confers with the salesman. The salesman does some calculating and hands me a slip of paper. I take it home, where the woman who promised to love, honor, and sign on my bottom line is waiting.

"The salesman says $600," I tell her. "What do you think?"

"Are you crazy?" she says. "Before he changes his mind, get back there and pay him."

# 8

## MOTHER NATURE LIVES HERE

Even if I could believe in Jim Anderson, there's no way I'm buying Margaret. How can anybody be expected to accept a woman whose dinner never burns, whose hair never moves, and who never falls asleep while her husband is telling her what happened to him at the office today?

I'll bet the woman never even called him at work.

In twenty years, I figure I have received roughly a million calls at work from the woman who promised to love, honor, and dial my number. Not one of them was to tell me that I'd won the Irish Sweepstakes, that a new Howard Hughes will had been discovered with my name on it, or that the rabbit lived. Instead, phone calls from home go something like:

ME: Hello, this is D.L. Stewart. Thank you for calling. How may I serve you today?

HER: It's me.

ME: Whaddya want?

HER: Just wait until you get home and see what your son did, that's what.

ME: Which son?

HER: The middle one.

ME: Is he the one that's seven?

HER: Eight.

ME: That's close enough. So, what has he done?

HER: He threw the cat into the basement clothes hamper.

ME: You called and interrupted me at work to tell me *that*? Being thrown into a clothes hamper certainly isn't going to hurt a cat.

HER: He threw it from the second floor.

ME: That's impossible.

HER: No it isn't. He dropped it down the clothes chute from the upstairs bathroom.

ME: Is the cat hurt?

HER: No.

ME: That's good.

HER: He's dead.

ME: Dead? What happened? Did he break his neck?

HER: He drowned.

ME: How could he have drowned from landing in a clothes hamper?

HER: He didn't drown from landing in the clothes hamper. He drowned after he jumped out of the clothes hamper and landed in the three feet of water.

ME: What three feet of water?

HER: The three feet of water that collected in the basement after the sump pump burned out.

ME: Good grief, that's terrible.

HER: Actually, the fireman said it could have been a whole lot worse.

ME: Well, thank goodness for . . . *Fireman*? What fireman?

HER: The one who came to put out the fire that started

when the sump pump burned out. The neighbors say he got here real fast.

ME: The neighbors say? Weren't you home?

HER: I wanted to be, but I had to go to school to pick up the thirteen-year-old.

ME: You mean in the middle of all this you went to school and took the thirteen-year-old out of class?

HER: Of course not. I took him out of the dispensary.

ME: Why was he in the dispensary?

HER: It's nothing serious. Just some nausea, dizziness, and vomiting. The school nurse said it's to be expected in cases like this.

ME: In cases like what?

HER: After a broken bone.

ME: What broken bone?

HER: Oh, didn't I tell you? He got into a fight with another kid at school and broke his arm.

ME: Well, I hope at least he gave a good account of himself. Is the other kid hurt much?

HER: I understand she got some nasty bruises on her knuckles.

ME: Let's get back to the fire in the basement. How much damage was there?

HER: I'm not exactly sure. The insurance agent came out, but he wouldn't give me an estimate because home-owners' policy doesn't cover flood damage. But, as I said before, the fireman pointed out that it could have been a lot worse. He said that it's a real good thing he had something to stand on top of so he could spray the water down on top of the sump pump.

ME: Well, that's something, anyway.

HER: It certainly is. I guess it's a good thing you spent all that money on a pool table, after all. Say, that reminds me. Did you know that firemen sometimes wear cleats?

ME: Uh, no, I didn't know that.

HER: Well, I guess that's all I have to tell you, so I

won't keep you any longer. I know you've got a lot on your mind. Bye bye.

Not only did Margaret never call Jim at the office, he probably never went ten rounds with her over a leaky dog crisis.

The leaky dog crisis happens on a day I have just spent eight hours hassling with an editor who seems to think that they have repealed the Emancipation Proclamation. Followed by a forty-five-minute drive home in ninety-two degree weather through traffic that would make Mario Andretti blanch. Not to mention twenty minutes looking for a parking spot near my house because there are so many bikes in the driveway it looks like the finish line for the Tour de France.

But at last I am in the comforting shelter of my little vine-covered cottage. And, as I walk through the garage door and into the kitchen, the woman who promised to love, honor, and poison my ivy greets me with: "Wait until you see what your dog did this morning."

Instantly, I know that I am in for a long evening. My dog is the one that scratches holes in the refrigerator door, eats the neighbor kids' Frisbees, and gets caught in sex movies with high government officials. The only time it's *our* dog is when it's just rescued a baby from a burning building, discovered the cure for cancer, or negotiated a Middle East peace settlement.

She leads me into the dining room and points to a large, wet spot on the rug.

"How do you like that?" she demands.

It is one of those questions for which there is no good answer. But I pause briefly to consider some possible responses:

(A) I don't like it.

(B) I do like it.

(C) It's OK, but I prefer neorealism.

"Well," I say, finally, "all day long I've been looking forward to coming home to something large and wet, but I was thinking more along the lines of a big pitcher of martinis."

"That's right, go ahead and make stupid jokes," she snaps.

"Why should you care if your stupid dog is ruining the house? What possible difference could it make to you that I work like a deckhand all day long to keep the place nice and she just goes around turning it into a cesspool that no self-respecting pig would be caught dead . . ."

"Wait a minute," I interrupt. "One wet spot on the dining room floor does not exactly make our street Tobacco Road. Besides, how can you be sure that she did it?"

"Who else would do it?"

"I don't know. Have you talked to the sixteen-year-old?"

"Don't be ridiculous. Of course it was the dog."

"The way I look at it, it's your word against hers. But, assuming it was her, what am I supposed to do about it? The horse is already out of the barn, so to speak."

"I don't know, but you'd better think of something."

"How about if I send her to her room without her supper?"

"I don't think that's going to do it."

"Ground her for the weekend."

"Try again."

"Take away her driving privileges?"

"C'mon, this is serious."

"All right, what about if we do what we used to do with the kids when we were toilet training them?"

"I don't think it's going to do much good to sit her on a potty chair with a coloring book."

"That's not what I meant. I'm talking about making sure she doesn't have anything to drink before she goes to bed."

"That might help," she concedes. "But, until we're sure the problem is taken care of, I think we should lock her in a room at night. At least that way there won't be spots all over the place."

It is, I have to agree, the best solution. And I know just which editor's office I'm going to lock her in, too.

The hostility between the dog and the woman who promised to love, honor, and scratch behind my ears is a major problem in our marriage. Which is puzzling, considering how she feels about other animals. I mean, I married Mother Nature.

Even before the wedding, I knew she had strong feelings for the birds of the air, the fish of the sea, and the beasts of the field. What I did not realize was that she felt personally responsible for every one of them. In twenty years, every stray cat this side of the Mississippi has spent a night on the rug next to our bed. Other people kill flies. At our house, they are captured, given a good meal, warned about the evils of indiscriminate sex, and sent on their way with good used clothing and money in their pockets.

But I didn't realize just what it was going to be like until the first time I tried to kill a spider in the kitchen of our first apartment.

As I remember it, I didn't even want to kill that spider. The way I felt about it, as long as he stayed out of my beer and didn't sit up all night with the television blaring, he could have lived there forever. But the woman who promised to love, honor, and come into my web begins to scream as soon as she sees him. So I walk into the kitchen, pick up a *Time* magazine and start to let him have it. And, in the middle of my backswing, she yells, "Wait, you're not going to kill him, are you?"

"Don't be silly," I reply. "I was just going to show him this article on Sino-Soviet relations and ask him what he thought of it. Of course I'm going to kill him. If you didn't want me to kill him, what was all the screaming about?"

"Well, he startled me, that's all. I don't want you to kill him, though."

"How about if I just give him a stern tongue-lashing and tell him he can't use the phone for the rest of the day?"

"What I mean is, can't you just sort of take him outside and let him go without hurting him?"

I scoop up the spider, take him out the front door, slip him a couple of bucks and tell him to be sure to write when he gets work.

That's just the beginning. When a mouse is discovered in

our garage, she stays up with it all night to protect it from the neighbor's cat. When I come home from fishing with a live catfish in my bait bucket, it winds up spending three weeks in our spare bedroom. Squirrels knock on our door every morning because she feeds them Macadamia nuts. Stray dogs have been discovered with maps to our house in their pockets.

One year, it's birds.

I learn about the birds when I come home from work to be greeted by the tantalizing smell of absolutely nothing cooking on the stove. I know she's home, though, because her checkbook is still warm. I locate her in the downstairs bedroom, peering out the window.

"Hey, I'm home," I say. "What's for dinner?"

"Shh," she whispers, "you'll disturb them."

"Disturb whom?"

"Them," she says, pointing to an overhang just outside the window, beneath which there are two birds nests. "Isn't it wonderful?"

"Terrific. Any day now we'll be hearing the patter of little claws in our backyard. Of course, I won't be able to hear them, because by that time I'll be too weak from hunger. So how about some dinner?"

"Sorry, I haven't had time to fix anything. Since I discovered them I've been too busy."

"Doing what, making maternity blouses?"

"No, watching them. The way they built those nests doesn't look very secure. I'm afraid that they might fall off the overhang and land on the patio."

"Well, that's between them and the building inspector. In the meantime, how about coming up and making something to eat?"

"Oh, all right. What would you like?"

"Scrambled eggs sounds good."

For the next two weeks she stations herself in the down-stairs bedroom, and I eat a lot of frozen dinners. Finally, one night, I am awakened by her hand shaking my shoulder.

"Wake up," she says, "I think the babies are being born."

"What do you want me to do," I mumble, "boil some water?"

"I just thought you'd like to get up and see it."

"I didn't want to get up when our babies were being born," I point out. "Come to think of it, neither did you."

But I get up, watch the baby birds being hatched, pass out some cigars, and go back to bed, telling myself that is that. You'd think by now I'd know better than to listen to myself. Because a few weeks later she walks into the living room cradling a baby robin in her hands.

"He's hurt. I think he fell out of the nest," she exclaims as she sets the bird gently on the rug. He staggers for a few steps and topples over onto his beak.

"Oh, I don't know," I say, "he could be stoned."

"Pick him up and bring him into the kitchen. I'll find a shoebox." While she goes off to look for a shoebox that is not full of petrified butterflies from last year's Cub Scout project, I hold the baby robin in my hands. It sits there quietly, its eyes closed. For an instant it crosses my mind that it may be dead. But then something warm and moist in the palm of my hand assures me that its bodily functions are still working.

By the time she gets back with the shoebox, the bird's bodily functions have worked half a dozen times, and my hands are starting to resemble the hood of a car that has been parked all night under a tree. I don't know what all is wrong with this bird, but it certainly is not constipation. She puts the bird into the shoebox and examines him.

"I think he's hungry," she says. She goes to the refrigerator, takes out a bunch of food, and spends the next twenty-five minutes fixing something for him to eat. Which is fifteen minutes more than she spent making dinner. Eventually, she has a mixture of milk, egg, and honey. Which, because we do not have an eye-dropper, we try to feed to him with a paper straw.

"I'll hold him and when he opens his beak, you pop some in there," she says.

I stand and wait for him to open his beak. After ten minutes I am beginning to suspect that his jaw is wired shut. But suddenly his beak falls open. I thrust the straw forward. By the time it gets there, his beak is shut and his head is turned. The mixture of milk, egg, and honey lands on the left side of his forehead and runs slowly down his face. Now, in addition to being injured, his left eye is glued shut.

For nearly an hour we work at getting food into him. It is messy work, but I know better than to suggest that perhaps this bird does not like milk, eggs, and honey and would prefer chewed–up worms like his mother used to make. Because I know who would get stuck doing the chewing.

When we have finished, she washes the bird, dries it off, listens while it says it prayers, tucks him in, and we all go to bed. The next thing I know, the first light of day is streaming in through the bedroom window and a loud, chirping sound is coming from the bathroom. I pry open one eye and look at the clock. It is 6:35. I get up and lurch into the bathroom. The woman who normally wouldn't get up before nine o'clock if her pillow was on fire is sitting on the edge of the tub. Feeding breakfast to the bird.

That afternoon she decides he has recovered enough to go back outside. We take him out into the backyard, set him free, and watch as he flutters away. As we go back into the house, there is a look of satisfaction on her face. She went to a lot of trouble for that bird, but obviously it was worth it to her.

I just hope he remembers to send her a card on Mother's Day.

No sooner has the bird flown out of our backyard than the lobster crawls into our lives.

The lobster joins us as a result of one of the traditions at our house, of which we have several. Each Christmas, for instance, we buy a tree that is three feet taller than our living room. Each Easter we hide eggs so well that at least one is never found until Memorial Day. Each Halloween I lose a quart of blood carving jack o'lanterns.

And on her birthday each year I cook dinner for the woman who promised to love, honor, and blow out my candles. Most years I stick pretty much to the basics: frozen pizza, Hamburger Helper, TV dinners, and other things with which our family is familiar. But on this year I decide to take a chance with her favorite food.

So on the afternoon of her birthday, I stop on my way home from work at a supermarket that has a tank of live lobsters. Although I never have cooked a live lobster before, I have read enough about them to know that when you pick one out, you should get one that is active. I peer into the tank. There are a dozen lobsters in the water, eleven of whom obviously are on Valium. The lone exception is a medium-sized lobster in the corner of the tank who is doing pushups. He has large claws, a plump body, and a hefty tail. To say nothing of pretty impressive biceps.

"I'll take that one," I tell the man who works in the seafood department. He reaches into the tank, pulls out the lobster just as it is getting ready to do some deep knee bends, and pops it into an empty plastic bag.

"Aren't you going to put him in water?" I ask. "I don't want him to die before I'm ready to cook him."

"Don't worry," the man says, "he'll last at least forty-five minutes without water. When you get him home, just put him in the refrigerator until you're ready."

I take the lobster and head for the cash register. It's a ten-minute drive home. That gives me, and the lobster, thirty-five minutes to spare. At the checkout area there are four cash registers open, three of which have long lines of people with overflowing shopping carts. At the fourth there is a lone lady carrying a box of Jell-O. I slip in behind her.

Fifteen minutes later the other three lines have disappeared and I still am standing there holding my lobster. It is the checkout girl's first day at the register. The lady has a coupon for ten cents off on Jell-O in her purse. Somewhere. And she

wants to pay for the Jell-O with a check. Drawn on the bank of
Hong Kong.

Finally, the lobster and I are out of the store. As we drive
out of the parking lot, we pass the lady with the Jell-O. I give
her a nasty look. The lobster flashes her an obscene gesture.

At home, I put the lobster on the top shelf of the refrigerator while I look for my cookbook. According to the cookbook,
there are two ways to kill a lobster. One is to put it, head first,
into a pot of boiling water. The other is to split it open by
inserting a sharp knife between its eyes. I decide to boil him. I
don't think I could stab an unarmed lobster.

When the water is boiling, I open the refrigerator. The
lobster has worked its way down to the third shelf. He has eaten
two apples, a dish of green beans, half a pound of bologna, and
he's working his way toward the leftover tuna-and-liver casserole. A couple of bites of that and I won't have to worry about
killing him. I take the lobster out of the refrigerator and carry
him to the stove. Just as I am about to drop him headfirst into
the pot, a familiar voice yells from the kitchen door.

"What are you doing?"

"I'm fixing your birthday dinner. It's an entire lobster, just
for you."

"But he's still alive," she exclaims.

"Of course. If you cook a lobster after it's dead, the meat
gets mushy."

"How can you bear to kill that poor thing? And how can
you expect me to eat something that was murdered in cold blood
in my own kitchen?"

"I wasn't going to tell you he was murdered. I was going to
tell you he slipped on the edge of the pot, hit his head, and
drowned."

"Well, just forget it. I'm not eating that lobster."

That evening we break tradition and have dinner at a
restaurant. Which is not too bad, actually, except that we have
to rush through dessert and hurry home. She's worried because
the lobster's at home all alone.

But living with a woman who acts like St. Francis of Assisi in a jogging suit is not the only thing that makes our relationship different from Jim and Margaret's. There also are the locks, the pills, and the notes.

First the locks.

I didn't know she was a lock fetishist when I married her. It's not the kind of question that necessarily comes up during your courtship. Besides, we didn't spend all that much time talking back then. So I don't discover that she has this compulsion for locking doors until we move into our first apartment.

"Darling?" she calls from the kitchen that first evening.

"Yes, sweetheart?" I call back.

"While I'm making dinner, would you be an angel and take out the garbage?"

"Certainly, my love."

I walk into the kitchen, where the garbage is sitting on the sink counter, next to the dinner she is preparing. It's easy to tell which is which. The garbage isn't burning. I pick up the bag, carry it outside, dump it into the trash bin, walk back to our apartment, and turn the door knob. It is locked.

"Hey," I yell, "the door's locked. Let me in."

"Who is it?" calls a voice from inside.

"Whaddya mean, who is it? It's me. Your beloved husband. You may remember me. I'm the guy who hasn't been heard from since he disappeared from our apartment three or four minutes ago."

"No need to be sarcastic," she says, unlocking the door to let me in.

"Well, what the heck did you lock the door for? I only went to the trash bin."

"Somebody could have come in and stolen our valuables," she says. "I would have been defenseless."

"We don't have any valuables," I point out. "Anyway, no one who can cook food that smells like that could ever be called defenseless." I'm not sure, but that may have been the moment the honeymoon ended.

Having come from a home where the only lock was on the liquor cabinet, being married to a lock fetishist takes a certain amount of adjustment. Each morning I would get up ten minutes before I was due at work, shower, shave, get dressed, throw open the front door, and sprint to my car. Each evening I would drive home from work, check the mail, try to guess where the paperboy threw the newspaper this time, go into the apartment, locate my tool box, and repair the chain lock that I had torn out of the door jamb that morning.

When we buy a house, it gets worse.

The same day we sign the final mortgage papers, she drives to the hardware store for locks. I carry them in from the car to the house. It takes four trips.

"What exactly are we going to do with all these locks?" I ask.

"Put them on the doors," she says.

"But, we only have three outside doors. There must be twenty-five locks here."

"We have more than three doors. There's the front door, the garage door, the patio door, the basement door, the . . ."

"Wait a minute. What basement door?"

"The one between the basement and the kitchen. If somebody breaks into the basement, a lock will keep them out of the kitchen."

"How is anybody supposed to break into the basement? There aren't any doors to it from outside. And the windows are walled over. The only way somebody could get into that basement is by digging a hole in the backyard, tunneling under the foundation, and blasting through the floor. Anybody who wants to do that isn't going to be too impressed by a $1.98 lock on a hollow door."

"I'll feel better if there's a lock on that door," she insists.

We put up the locks. All twenty-five of them. There are three locks on the front door. Two on the garage door. Two on the patio door. Four on the medicine chest door. A couple on the refrigerator door. We may have the only house on the block with a lock on the fireplace screen. If the Watergate offices had had this many locks on its doors, Bernstein and Woodward would be covering garden club meetings today.

All those locks, I'll have to admit, do give me a certain sense of security. A professional burglar still could get in, but it probably would take him about an hour to do it. Heck, it takes almost that long to get out.

Like her preoccupation with locks, I had no way of knowing before we were married that she would turn out to be a drug pusher. For the first few months after we are married, in fact, the only medicine I ever saw in our apartment was a bottle of aspirin and some little white pills that came out of a little round plastic dispenser with some numbers on it.

But then we started having babies, and the little round plastic dispenser got pushed to the back of the medicine chest behind an ever-growing collection of capsules, tablets, and syrups. The delivery car from the pharmacy wore out three clutches and a transmission bringing prescriptions to our house. Revco asked us about the possibility of a merger.

Most of the pills went into the kids.

A ten-year-old would come in after four hours of touch football with a drop of sweat on his forehead, and she would pop a pill into his mouth because she was sure he had a fever. If a seven-year-old dared to clear his throat in the middle of the night, she had a quart of medicine in him before dawn.

Which is not to say that she handed out medicine indiscriminately. She had read enough medical books to graduate magna cum laude from Johns Hopkins. My favorite author is Charles Dickens. Hers is Lendon Smith.

Fortunately, I have been fairly healthy most of my life, and she hasn't had much of a chance to practice medicine on me. But one day I make a big mistake. I sneeze twice in her presence.

"I don't like the sound of that," she says, taking off her stethoscope. "I think maybe you're coming down with something. Probably a cold."

"I doan hab a code," I say.

"Aha," she exclaims.

Before I can get my hanky to my nose, she has a thermom-
eter in my mouth, a hand on my brow, and every medication
this side of Ex–Lax on the table next to me.

"We'd better start with this," she says, thrusting a bottle of
yellow liquid at me.

"Whad is id?" I ask.

"Triaminic," she says. "It's just your basic phenylpro-
panolamine hydrochloride, pheniramine maleate, pyrilamine
maleate, and guaifenesin." To a man who doesn't know Midol
from Maalox, that's not really a great deal of help.

"Whad does id do?"

"It's an expectorant. It will help you cough."

I point out to her that if I really do have a cold, I probably
will not need much help coughing. She explains to me that if I
don't take two spoons of Triaminic immediately, my cold could
lead to an upper respiratory infection, bronchitis, and, possibly,
pneumonia. Before she can get to the part about how I probably
am only one step ahead of malaria, typhoid, and bubonic plague,
I take two slugs of the yellow stuff.

Two hours later, I am no longer sneezing. I am too busy
coughing.

"It's time for some of this," she says, handing me a bottle
of green stuff. "It's Novahistine, to keep your nose from
running."

I start to mention that, if it wasn't for my nose running, I
wouldn't be getting any exercise at all. But I decide to save my
breath for coughing. I take two swigs of the green stuff.

By bedtime she has pumped enough liquid medicine into
me to drown Mark Spitz and has made me pop more pills than an
NFL linebacker. If I manage to survive this cold, I figure Eli
Lilly will name me its man of the year. Not that I'm complaining, you understand. I know she has only my best interests
at heart. But I can't help but wonder how I made it through the
colds of my childhood, when all my mother did was hand me a

box of Smith Brother's cough drops, rub my chest with chicken soup, and send me to bed.

The locks and pills have been with us only for as long as we have been married. The notes have been in our lives even longer, all the way back to the night I popped THE question.

It is a clear spring evening. We are sitting in my car in front of her house. In the living room, I can see her parents. Her mother is sitting on the couch. She is a small woman, capable of sympathetic understanding for young lovers. Her father is sitting in an easy chair. He is a big man, capable of crushing a trifling suitor with his bare hands.

The night air is cool, but there is perspiration on my forehead as I turn to her. My throat is dry. My stomach is nervous. I gaze into her eyes.

"Darling? I have something to ask you."

"Yes?"

"Would you? That is, could you? I mean, will you . . ."

"Just a minute, sweetheart," she interrupts, reaching into her purse. She pulls out a pen and a piece of paper. She writes something on the paper, then puts them back into her purse.

"Now then," she says, "what was it you were saying?"

It is my first clue that I have become involved with a note addict. But it is just a taste of what is to come.

There is, for instance, our wedding day, when the minister asks if she will love, honor, and cherish and she looks at him and says softly, "Do you have a pen I can borrow?"

There is our wedding night, when she calls down to room service for a scratch pad.

There is our trip to Europe, during which she writes notes to herself at the foot of the Eiffel Tower, the top of Notre Dame, inside the Coliseum, and outside the Vatican. Other tourists came home with paintings, statues, French berets, and Italian silk ties blessed by the Pope. We came home with twenty-two pounds of excess notepaper.

At first, most of her writing goes on a little piece of paper, which she carries in her purse. I take a look at it one day. It is

filled with messages, shopping lists, chores for me to do, sales for
her not to miss, relatives' birthdays, friends' birthdays, strangers' birthdays, presidents' birthdays, and enough phone numbers to fill the Manhattan Yellow Pages. All of which is scribbled
on a piece of notebook paper no bigger than three by five inches.
Give her two index cards and she could transcribe *War and
Peace.*

Then her writing starts to spread. One day she picks me up
from work. As I slide behind the wheel of the car, I notice a tiny
scrap of paper taped to the dashboard. The word "gas" is written
on it.

"Is this some kind of warning about dinner?" I ask.

"It's to remind me that the car is almost out of gas," she
says.

We drive home. In the kitchen there is a piece of paper
taped to the refrigerator.

"That's to remind me that we're almost out of milk," she
says.

I walk into the living room. There is a piece of paper taped
to the phone.

"That's to remind me to call my mother," she says.

I walk into the bedroom. There is a piece of paper taped to
my pillow.

"Relax," she says. "That's to remind me to turn the
mattress."

After twenty years of living with a note junkie, it's obvious
to me that she never will kick the habit. It's not even worth
talking about. But, one night, we are looking back on those
early days, reminiscing about the time when our bills and my
stomach both were much smaller.

"Remember the night when I asked you to marry me?"

"Of course."

"Well, there's one thing I've always wondered. Just as I was
about to ask you, you took a piece of paper out of your purse
and wrote a note to yourself. Remember that?"

"Sure."

"Do you remember what you wrote?"

"Certainly. In fact, I still have the note."

She reaches into her purse and pulls out a piece of paper. It is wrinkled and yellow. Carefully, she unfolds it. She hands it to me. Written in a clear, firm hand are the words: "Buy more notepaper."

After twenty years of stray birds, locked doors, and note-scribbling, she decides that it is time for her to go back to college. It is a decision for which she has my whole-hearted support. Sort of.

On the one hand, what could be more American than the concept of an eighties woman successfully managing a home and family, while at the same time furthering her education and expanding her intellectual horizons? On the other hand, I keep wondering why the first course she elects to take is abnormal psychology.

A few weeks after her class starts, I ask her about it.

"May I ask you a question?" I say.

"Open communication is the key to healthy interpersonal relationships," she says. "As Sachs and Neville pointed out in their 1974 study of tribal verbalizations among adolescents in the South Fiji Island . . . "

"A simple yes or no would be enough."

"Yes."

"It's about you going back to school."

"It bothers you, doesn't it?  You resent the fact that I refuse to spend the rest of my life cooped up in the kitchen. You've probably got some smart remark about how, since I started to take that psychology course, all my meat loaves have come out of the oven looking like Rorschach tests."

"Actually, they're starting to taste like Rorschach tests. But that's not what's bothering me, and I really don't resent your going back to school. After all, it's only fair, since you supported me when I was a senior in college."

"I'm glad you remember that. Those were three pretty tough years."

"I remember. But what I really wanted to ask was, why did you pick abnormal psychology?"

"The nuclear physics class was full."

"Come on, you know what I mean. Why didn't you take something with a more practical application? Something that would help us in our day-to-day living?"

"You mean like plumbing?"

"I was thinking more of something like child psychology."

"What's so practical about child psychology?"

"Maybe you could find a way to keep the eleven-year-old from trying to stuff his brother into the microwave. Or learn how to get the sixteen-year-old not to leave his tennis shoes on top of the television."

"If I was interested in getting the sixteen-year-old to pick up after himself, I wouldn't go to college. I'd go to Lourdes."

"You're probably right. But at least a course like that would give us some help in raising the kids."

"I did consider that," she admits. "But, the more I thought about it, the more I realized that child psychology would be useful only for a limited time. In a few years the kids would be grown up and gone, and then what use would child psychology be to me?"

"Wait a minute, I don't think I like the way this conversation is headed. What you're saying is that after the kids are gone, abnormal psychology still will be useful to you because the only one left in the house will be me. I resent that."

"There seems to be a certain amount of hostility in your voice," she says.

"Maybe there is."

"Would you like to lie down on the couch and tell me about it?"

"No, I don't want to lie down on the couch. And stop stroking your beard."

"I'm merely rubbing my chin," she says. "Besides, you're getting all worked up over nothing. The only reason I picked this course is because it interests me and it's something I can use toward my degree."

Despite her assurances, I am not entirely convinced. Something tells me that the only reason she took abnormal psychology was because she knew she wouldn't have to leave the house to come up with material for a term paper.

Going back to school is her idea. Going back to work is not. Mostly because she is blessed with a selective memory. Because we made a lot of promises to each other before we were married.

"Every day will be heaven," I vowed.

"Every night will be paradise," she pledged.

"We never will argue," I insisted.

"We never even will think of disagreeing," she declared.

"No wife of mine will ever have to go to work," I swore.

After twenty years of heaven, the only promise she distinctly remembers is the one about her never having to go to work. Which might not be a problem if it wasn't that our income has a tough time keeping up with our outgo. Our checkbook would be written in red ink, if we could afford red ink.

"I thought you said last year was going to be a good one for us," she says when I mention the subject of her getting a part-time job to help pay some of the bills. "What happened to all that money you said you were going to make in 1983?"

"We spent it in 1978."

"Well, maybe we should talk to someone about our financial situation."

"Who? The only one who could understand our financial situation would be the Social Security Administration. I'm telling you, we have a real problem."

"Just simmer down. There's no sense getting all worked up over a few thousand dollars."

"A few thousand dollars? We owe more than that to the paper boy. I'm talking major–league debt, here. Not even Ronald Reagan would try to balance this budget. It's obvious that there are going to have to be some drastic changes in our money picture."

"All right, from now on I'll cut you back to one sandwich in your lunch."

"That's not what I had in mind. I was talking about you going out and finding a job."

"A job? You promised me that I would never have to go to work. Besides, if I did get a job, I wouldn't want to do it until after the kids were big enough to stay in the house by themselves after school."

"What are you talking about? Those kids are big enough to *lift* the house by themselves."

Reluctantly, she agrees to start looking for a job soon. "Soon" comes and goes. "After a while" slips past. "One of these days" becomes a blurred memory. Eventually, we arrive at "in the distant future."

"I thought you were going to get a job," I remind her, finally.

"Don't rush me," she says. "I'm waiting for the right thing to come along."

"I hate to tell you this, but all the cushy jobs are filled already. At least until the next elections. I'd suggest that you start looking in the want ads."

"I tried that. Unless I want to get into sales, which I don't, the only openings are for a go–go girl or an overhead–garage–door installer."

"I think you'd make a terrific overhead–garage–door installer."

Several days later I come home from work to find her standing behind a pile of new skirts and blouses stacked on the bed.

"Guess what?" she says. "I've found a job."

"Doing what, hijacking clothing delivery trucks?"

"No, it's a part–time office job. But I'll need this many clothes for work."

"Diana Ross doesn't need that many clothes for work."

But now I have a working wife. Half as much room in the

closet for my clothes. And a guilty conscience about breaking that promise.

But at least we've kept all the other ones.

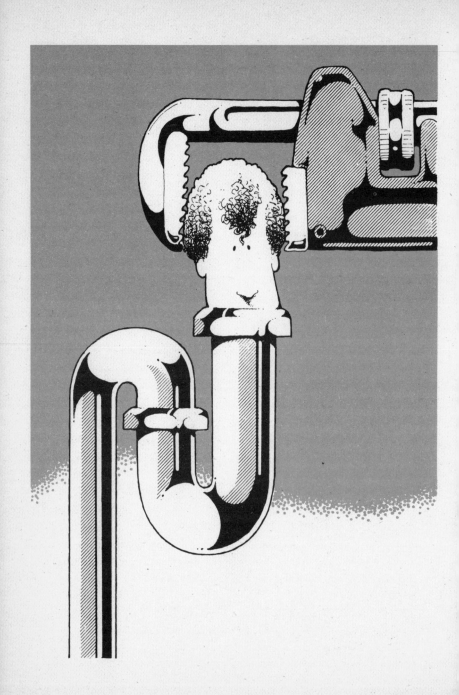

# 9

## THE GRASS OVER MY SEPTIC TANK IS DEAD

So she's not exactly Jane Wyatt. On the other hand, I'm not necessarily Robert Young.

For every Swiss steak she has put on the table that would turn Julia Child into a vegetarian, there's a leaky faucet in our house that I've been trying to fix since 1978. If her living room doesn't look like the cover of *House Beautiful*, it could be because some of the wallpaper I put up last fall still is sticking to the picture window.

The tough jobs around the house don't bother me. It's the little ones that make me break out in a rash. If I had to, I imagine I could put together a nuclear reactor in an hour or two. But moving a curtain rod over about three inches is a lifetime job. Splitting the atom is a snap compared to keeping the toilet from running all night. Why did I waste my time taking two semesters of English lit when I could have been learning something useful? Like learning how to fix a doorknob.

But, like most people, I always used to take doorknobs for granted. Through a lifetime of broken lawn mowers, clanging refrigerators and washing machines that jogged through the laundry room, the doorknob has been the one reliable fixture around our house. It does its job through wind, rain, snow, and power failure. General Motors never has recalled it. Ralph Nader never has put a seat belt on it. It is one of the few things the Surgeon General has yet to test to see how many you have to eat before it causes cancer. The only thing in our house less breakable is my bowling ball.

That's why I am so unprepared when the eleven-year-old calls me at work in the middle of the afternoon and says, "Mom says to tell you that the bathroom doorknob is broken."

"Which one?"

"The one with the blonde hair and glasses and . . ."

"Which bathroom?"

"Oh. The upstairs one. It's broken real bad."

"Define 'real bad.' "

"It's sitting on the floor in the hall outside the bathroom."

"So why didn't Mom call to tell me about this herself?"

"She's sitting on the floor inside the bathroom."

"Tell her I'll be right home."

"She said to take your time. She said this is the first time she's been alone in there for more than 10 minutes since the stretch marks started. What does that mean?"

"Beats me."

When I get home that evening, the woman who promised to love, honor, and share my tub is in the kitchen.

"I see you were able to break out of the bathroom," I say.

"The eight-year-old broke in," she says.

"I wonder why the doorknob fell off? Do you think it was the sixteen-year-old pulling on it? He's pretty rough with things."

"Don't be silly. The sixteen-year-old hasn't closed a door in four years. Besides, I already asked him and he denied it. He's blaming it on the eleven-year-old."

"What does the eleven-year-old say?"

"He's blaming it on the eight-year-old."

"What does the eight-year-old say?"

"He says we should check the knob for dog paw prints."

"Maybe we've been jumping to conclusions and the door-knob actually died of natural causes. Maybe it's supposed to fall off at this time of year and if we wait until spring, the door will grow a new one."

"I don't think so. You're going to have to fix it."

I agree to fix it. But only because there are no listings for "doorknob repairmen" in the Yellow Pages.

At first glance, fixing a doorknob looks like something that even I can do. All I'll have to do is push the outside half of the doorknob back into the hole in the door, push the inside half of the knob into the other side of the hole in the door, and squeeze them together. I should be back in front of the television before the basketball game starts.

I slide the outside half into the hole in the door, push the inside half against it, and step back to admire my work. Which is the only thing that keeps my foot from being badly bruised by the falling doorknob. I may miss the opening tip-off.

I try again, pushing a little harder this time to make sure it stays. Satisfied that it finally is fixed, I flip off the bathroom light. Which is why I only *hear* the doorknob fall into the tub. I may miss the whole first half.

The problem, apparently, is that I am not lining up the two halves of the doorknob correctly. But, obviously, I can't be on both sides of the door at the same time to align them. So I compromise. I sit on the bathroom floor with one leg and one eye on each side of the door and half a knob in each hand, trying to slide them together. It is beginning to look as if I am going to miss the basketball game, the playoffs, the championship finals, and most of the baseball season.

Just as my eyes are starting to become permanently crossed from trying to slide the two halves together, the eight-year-old appears in the hall. He is jumping up and down.

"I didn't realize that watching a man fix a doorknob was so exciting," I say.

"It's not exciting, Dad," he says jumping up and down a little faster. "I hafta go."

"Use the one downstairs. I've almost got this doorknob together. I can't let go of it now or I'll have to start all over."

"There's a big line downstairs and I can't wait. I hafta go real, real bad." By now he is jumping up and down like Michael Jackson with an overdose of caffeine.

"Oh, all right, just climb over me and go in."

He climbs over my shoulder into the bathroom. And then stands there.

"Too late?" I ask.

"I can't go while you're watching." This is the same kid who, when he was two, couldn't wait for company to come so he could tear off his diaper and run into the living room to do his springer spaniel imitation.

"I'm not watching," I tell him.

"You're listening."

"I'm not listening."

"Promise?"

"I promise."

"If you're not listening, how could you hear me ask you if you promised?"

With a sigh, I get up off the floor and let the doorknob fall out of the hole in the door. The inside half hits the linoleum, skips once and takes a chip out of the bathtub. The outside half bounces into the hall, down the steps, and out of my sight into the foyer, where it comes to a stop with a loud clunk.

My guess is that it broke my bowling ball.

After 20 years of losing battles like that, I have arrived at certain conclusions about being a homeowner: The grass is always greener over my neighbor's septic tank. A man who says he likes to spend his weekends puttering about the house will lie about other things, too.

And the heaviest thing in the world is an eighty-pound bag of water-softener salt.

I learn about water-softener salt on the day we buy our

first house, a three-bedroom ranch with wall-to-wall carpeting in the living room, 1½ baths, a 1½ car garage, and a mortgage that is going to take 1½ lifetimes to pay off. Ten minutes after I sign the papers, a water-softener salesman is on the phone.

"When do you want your water softener delivered?" he asks.

"Who said I want a water softener?"

"Everybody who lives in your plat needs a water softener. The water out there is very hard."

"So what? I wasn't planning on throwing it at anybody."

"You don't understand. When you have hard water, mineral deposits build up in your pipes. After a while they'll be completely clogged. It's as if your house was developing hardening of the arteries. You know what will happen then, don't you?"

"My house will have a heart attack?"

"Not exactly. But your pipes will burst. Imagine what that would be like."

I imagine what that would be like. My pipes clogging. My pipes bursting. My wall-to-wall carpeting floating. I order a water softener.

A week later, the woman who promised to love, honor, and man my lifeboat says that the water softener needs to have salt put into it.

"Well, go ahead and put it in, then. I'm watching the ballgame."

"The bag weighs eighty pounds," she says. "Of course, if it's too much trouble for you to get out of your chair, I suppose I could get the lady next door to help me. Or I could have the four-year-old stand on a chair while I lift . . ."

"Oh, all right, I'll do it," I say. She gets so crabby when she's pregnant.

I go out into the garage, where two eighty-pound bags of salt have been left by the delivery man. I bend over, grab one end of a bag, and lift. When the bag is approximately as high as my knees, the salt inside shifts to the other end. The bag slips from my hands and lands approximately on my foot. I wriggle my foot out from underneath the bag, grab it in the middle, and lift again. The salt inside shifts to both ends. I wriggle both feet out from under the bag.

I bend down, grab both ends of the bag, grunt like a Russian weightlifter, and hoist the bag up to my shoulder. Now I know why Russian weightlifters grunt. It helps drown out the popping noises in their backs.

Clinging to the bag with both hands, I stagger to the kitchen door. Which is closed. I can't open the door because I need both hands to balance the bag. I shift my weight to compensate for the eighty pounds on my shoulder, balance on one foot, and kick the door with the other.

"Stop kicking that door or I'll tell your father," a voice from inside the kitchen shouts.

"I *am* her father," I shout. "Open the door."

She opens the door. I stagger to the laundry room and locate the water softener. It's the one with the lid on it. I can't lift the lid, because I need both hands to hold the bag. If I put the bag on top of the tank, I won't be able to lift the lid. If I put the bag on the floor while I lift the lid, I'll have to hoist the bag again.

"How about coming in here and taking off this lid for me?" I shout.

She comes in and takes off the lid. All I have to do now is pour in the salt. As soon as I cut the bag open.

"Would you bring me a knife?" I shout.

"Steak knife or butter knife?"

"Who cares what kind of knife? Just get it in here. I'm already four inches shorter than I was when I started."

She brings the knife. I cut the bag. I pour the salt. A lot of it lands in the tank. A lot of it almost lands in the tank. A lot of it doesn't land within walking distance of the tank. At this point I don't really care very much. Because I know that as long as we own a house in the suburbs, there are going to be lawns that need mowing, walls that need papering, faucets that need washering, kids that need car pooling, and water softeners that need salting.

And, at that moment, I have a pretty good idea who's going to spend the rest of his life holding the bag.

On those rare occasions I don't have my hands full holding the bag, it's usually because they're busy going into something. Like into toilets to rescue dolls that can walk, talk, wet, roller skate, and cruise singles bars but can't swim. Or into garbage disposals that are filled with coffee grounds, egg shells, potato peels, and contact lenses. Not only have I given up trying to guess where my hands are going next, I am doing my best to forget about where they've been.

But, no matter how hard I try, it's tough to forget about the day I come home from work and find five T-shirts and a Little League athletic supporter hanging from the kitchen light fixture.

"I love what you've done with the place," I say to the woman who promised to love, honor, and decorate my life. "Is it something you saw in *Better Homes and Gardens*?"

"Very cute," she snaps. "But I'm in no mood for smart remarks. I've been hanging clothes over anything that gives off heat ever since the dryer broke down this afternoon leaving me with twenty pounds of wet wash and no place to take it because you had the car. If I don't get everything dry pretty soon, you'll be going to work tomorrow in the very latest in designer mildew."

"What seems to be the problem with the dryer?"

"It spins around, but it won't heat. I called the repair place, but they can't send anyone out for three days. The guy there said we should check the exhaust vent at the side of the house. He said it's possible that an animal crawled up in there for warmth and has it blocked. I was waiting for you to get home so you can stick your hand up in there and check it."

"You don't seriously expect me to stick my hand in some place where a wild animal might be hiding," I say.

"It's not as if I'm asking you to arm wrestle a mountain

lion," she replies. "If there is an animal in there, it's probably just a frightened little rabbit trying to keep warm."

"If it's just a frightened little rabbit, why don't you put your hand in there?"

"I just did my nails."

"Well, I don't really feel like poking around in some place where an animal is holed up. Any animal can be dangerous when it's cornered. What if it bites off my typing finger?"

"OK, suit yourself, Grizzly Adams," she says. "Oh, by the way, if you're going upstairs, hang these bras on the hall light. And check your stereo receiver and see if my pantyhose are dry yet. If they are, I can take them off and drape some wet sheets over it. Those should dry in a couple of days."

"All right, all right, I get the message. I'll check the vent after dinner. Speaking of which, what's that you've got going in the oven?"

"Three pounds of damp socks."

"I thought it smelled better than usual."

After dinner, which we eat standing up because all the dining room chairs are straddling furnace registers with wet shirts hanging over them, I take the dog and go outside to check the exhaust vent. When it comes to wild animals, the dog is not a great deal braver than I am. But if I can convince her that there's a newspaper boy holed up in there, she'll bark it to death.

Warily, I approach the vent. It is a cylinder made of thin, galvanized steel that sticks out of the wall about six inches above the ground. When I get within fifteen feet, I stop. I figure that's close enough to hear if there's anything in there growling.

I don't hear anything, so I call the dog and point my finger toward the vent. Alertly, she runs up and sniffs my finger. Not only am I probably going to get my finger bitten off, I am probably going to get it bitten off by my own dog. Before she can open her mouth, I grab her by the collar and drag her to the vent, pushing her nose to the opening.

Her canine instincts, still deeply inbred despite generations of domesticity, take over, and she does what nature has taught her to do. After she does what nature has taught her to do, she scratches up some grass to cover it and trots away.

By now it's really too dark to feel if there's anything hiding up inside the exhaust vent, so I give up and go back into the house. Living in a house decorated with originals by Fruit of the Loom isn't that bad. Besides, there's still plenty of room in the crock pot.

For some reason, I assumed that problems like that would go away when we moved into our brand-new house. A new house, after all, should be perfect. If for no other reason than that I haven't had a chance to mess anything up. But even new houses pose challenges. For one thing, they don't come with mailboxes.

Which is something I do not know until a few weeks after we move in and the woman who promised to love, honor, and cancel my stamps asks if I've noticed that it's been quite some time since the mailman has stopped by.

"Now that you mention it, I did notice that," I say. "Do you think it's something we said?"

"Of course not. It's because we don't have a mailbox."

"That's silly. All houses have mailboxes."

"New ones in the suburbs don't."

So I go out and buy a mailbox at a department store. Because we live on a new street, all mailboxes on our block are put up side-by-side on the same curbside stand. Unfortunately, the stand is located in the middle of the block, fifty yards from our house. Fortunately, I am in good shape and the drive does not tire me too much.

A few weeks after I put up our mailbox, a man rings our doorbell.

"Hello," he says, "I'm from the post office."

"Can you prove that?" I ask.

"Beg pardon?"

"Can you prove that you're from the post office. I mean, how do I know that you're really from the post office and not just saying that so you can get a foot in the door to sell me aluminum siding?"

"I don't have any credentials, if that's what you mean."

"Well, then, what branch of the post office are you from?"

"Downtown."

"How long did it take you to get to our house from there?"

"Four days."

"I'm convinced."

The man from the post office explains that next week the mail service will be extended the entire length of the street, which means that each house must have a mailbox in front of it. A lot of people, he says, are working in cooperation, putting the post on the property line between houses and attaching two mailboxes to it.

The next morning my neighbor and I meet at the property line. He has brought a post, a shovel, a post-hole digger, a crowbar, two bags of cement, a wheelbarrow, a carpenter's level, a hammer, a box of nails, and a garden hose. Noah built an ark with less than that.

We agree on a spot for the hole and start digging. The first jab of the shovel into the ground is met with a thud that sends vibrations up to my wrists.

"Must have hit a rock. I'll try a different spot."

I try a different spot. There is another thud, which sends vibrations into my forearms. Four more spots bring four more thuds and have my entire upper body vibrating like a '53 Ford.

"Maybe we'd better use the post-hole digger," my neighbor says. While he digs with the post-hole digger, I pour the cement into the wheelbarrow, add the water, and begin to mix it.

"The cement's all ready," I announce after several minutes of mixing. "How's the hole coming?"

"Pretty well," he says. "All I have to do is get it thirty-eight inches deep."

"How deep is it now?"

"About two inches."

I keep stirring the cement. My neighbor keeps digging. After an hour he has gone down six inches, and my shoulders are aching.

"I'm going to stop stirring," I say.

"You can't do that," he says.

"Why not? Will that cause problems?"

"It will unless you know somebody who needs a block of cement shaped like the inside of a wheelbarrow."

We decide to trade jobs. After another hour of digging, the hole is twenty inches deep. We have found either the world's hardest dirt or the world's softest diamonds. At twenty-five inches, I am sick of digging.

"This is close enough," I say, "let's just put the post in now."

"We can't," he says. "The box would be too high. Postal regulations say it has to be between forty and forty-four inches above street level. It's a Federal thing."

I resume digging. The last thing I want is to wind up in Leavenworth on a too-tall mailbox rap. Finally, the hole is thirty-eight inches deep. We stick the post into it. We shovel the cement into the hole around it.

"Well, that's that," I say. "Let's go have a beer."

"Are you crazy? We can't just leave it. It's got to be supported overnight so the cement can harden. Otherwise it might tip."

"I'll send a kid out to hold it. The fifteen-year-old is always nagging me to let him stay out all night."

"No need for that. We'll just brace it with these two by fours."

He begins driving pieces of wood into the ground, connecting them to other pieces of wood and then connecting those pieces of wood to pieces of wood attached to the mailbox. By the time he has finished, there is more wood supporting my mailbox than there is supporting my house.

"That should hold it in case it gets hit by a strong wind," he says.

"That should hold it in case it gets hit by a Pershing missile," I say.

The next morning I go out to the mailbox. Not only is the cement dry but the post is perfectly straight. And in the mailbox is an envelope. Our first letter.

I open it up and take it out. It is a bill from the department store. For the mailbox.

Once the mailbox is in, I figure I have done about all the work I am going to have to do around our new house. A week later, the woman who promised to love, honor, and dim my bulb decides that we need a lamppost in our front yard.

"We're the only ones on the block without a lamppost in our front yard," she points out. "How are people supposed to find our place at night?"

"Simple. Tell them to look for the only house on the block that's dark," I reply.

"What about burglars? What's going to happen if a crook comes along some night when we're not home and finds the place all dark?"

"I know exactly what's going to happen. He's going to take three steps into the yard, fall over a Big Wheel, land in a pile of bikes, get up, twist his ankle on a soccer ball, and catch it right in the throat from a badminton net that hasn't been put away since Lyndon Johnson."

"OK," she concedes, "I really think we need a lamppost in our front yard, but if you don't want one, I won't push it. It's entirely up to you. I'll go along with whatever you decide. You are, after all, the lord of the house and the king of the castle."

"It's nice of you to be so understanding. I guess I could consider putting one in sometime."

"Good. It's in the garage."

"What is?"

"The lamppost. I bought it three days ago."

I adjust my robe, pick up my crown, and walk to the garage, where the lamppost is waiting to be installed. Basically, all I know about installing a lamppost is that you need a lamppost, a bulb, some wire, and a hole in the ground. I open the box and examine the contents. It contains a lamppost, a bulb, and some wire. Just as I feared. The hole in the ground is not included.

I point this out to the woman who promised to love, honor, and help me shovel it.

"Of course there's no hole," she says. "You have to dig that yourself."

"Do you have any idea what it's like to dig a hole in our yard? The ground is like granite."

"Well, I'm sure you can do it, dear," she says, getting into her car and driving off to the store.

Four hours, three shovels, two post-hole diggers, and a permanently twisted back later, there is an eighteen-inch hole in our front yard near the end of the driveway. The next step is to mix the cement to put into the hole. I pick up the sixty-pound bag of ready-mix cement. It weighs 400 pounds. I pour thirty pounds into a wheelbarrow, twenty pounds onto my shoe, and ten pounds onto a patch of grass that never will be green again.

Next I hook up a garden hose that has spent the entire winter in the garage tangling itself. I squirt water into the wheelbarrow and stir with a shovel for several minutes. Eventually, I have a mixture that reminds me of her pancake batter. Only not so heavy.

Time is important now, because the cement mixture sets quickly. I put the post into the hole. I stick the shovel into the wheelbarrow full of cement. The phone rings.

The only ones home are me and the dog. I look at the dog. She is busy eyeing the post. I race into the house and pick up the phone. A voice at the other end congratulates me and says that I have been selected as a very special family to preview a new concept in encyclopedias. I tell the voice what it can do with volumes I through IX. I slam down the phone and race back to the wheelbarrow. The shovel still is in it. Sticking straight up.

I pry the shovel loose and scoop enough cement into the

hole to support the lamppost. By the time I have finished, it is too dark to do any more work. I clean out the wheelbarrow, hang up my tools, retangle the garden hose, and go into the house to wash up. As I am standing at the sink, cleaning cement from underneath my fingernails, I hear a familiar-sounding car coming up the street. The car slows down in front of our house. It pulls into the driveway. Then there is another sound. It is the sound of metal on metal.

The impulse to run outside and see what she hit passes quickly. There is only one possibility.

Even with cement hardening on the lawn and a lamppost bending in the breeze, the yard surrounding our new house is attractive. In fact, one of the reasons we bought the house was because it came on a lovely, wooded lot, with two stately elm trees in the front and nearly 100 little maples in the back.

Three weeks after we move in, the stately elm trees die.

"Probably blight," the real estate agent guesses.

"I assumed it wasn't a double suicide," I reply. "The question is, what are you going to do about it?"

"Gosh, there's not much I can do. Sorry."

After a year and a half, the 100 maple trees in the back still are little, the two elm trees in the front still are dead, and we're getting a lot of flak from the neighbors. Having a front yard in which the only two trees are posthumous probably wouldn't matter so much if we lived in a different neighborhood. But the guy across the street is one of those landscaping freaks whose ambition in life is to recreate the Versailles gardens in his front yard. Then there's the couple next door: Mr. and Mrs. Luther Burbank.

But the biggest complaints come from the woman who promised to love, honor, and prune my branches.

"You can't just let dead trees stand there forever," she insists.

"I don't see why not. In the winter, they look exactly like all the other trees. Besides, what proof do you have that they're really dead and not just dormant?"

"Neither of them has had a leaf on it for almost two years."

"You call that proof?"

"What do you want, a coroner's report and Billy Graham standing in our front yard delivering a eulogy? I'm telling you, those stupid trees are dead, and you're going to have to do something about it."

"How about if we just wait a little bit longer? Eventually the fifteen-year-old is bound to run over them with the rider mower."

"Suit yourself. But one of these days one of those stupid trees is going to fall over."

"I'm not worried."

"On top of the garage."

"No big deal."

"While your new car is parked inside."

I place some calls to see how fast I can get someone to come out and take down those stupid trees. By the time they finish quoting prices for trimming, felling, cutting, and hauling, I calculate that I would be better off letting them fall on my new car. With me sitting at the wheel.

I mention my problem to the guy across the street.

"As a matter of fact, I have a tree in my front yard that has to come down, too," he says. "Why don't we save a lot of money and do it ourselves?"

"That sounds sort of risky," I say. "What if they fall the wrong way and land on our houses?"

"Hey, there's nothing to it," he says.

"Are you sure?" I ask.

"Positive," he says.

"Well, if you think we can do it . . ."

"Great," he says. "We'll do yours first."

On Saturday morning he shows up in my front yard with a chain saw and 100 feet of yellow nylon rope. We're going to loop the rope around the tree and pull on it to make sure it falls the right way, he explains.

We loop the yellow rope around the tree, he hands one end

to me, and tells me to walk out into the street and pull it taut while he saws. I walk out into the street with the rope in my hand. By now I am starting to have second thoughts about this whole operation. If cutting down a tree is so simple, why did those companies want to charge me so much to do it? If he's so sure he can make the tree fall the way he wants it to, why aren't we doing the one in front of his house first?

But it is too late to turn back. He already is starting to saw into the tree. I pull as hard as I can on the rope to make sure the tree doesn't fall on my house. Suddenly, I realize that if the tree starts to fall the wrong way, I never will be able to hold onto the rope. I have a mental picture of the rope sliding through my hands. The tree falling on top of my large suburban house. Me becoming the owner of two small suburban houses.

In a burst of inspiration, I decide to tie the rope around my waist. While he continues to saw, I quickly loop the rope around my waist and tie it securely. The instant I have finished the knot, I have another mental picture. The tree falling the wrong way with me tied to it. Me catapulting over my large suburban house. Frantically, I untie the knot.

Just as I get it untied, the tree begins to fall. With a loud crack and a mighty crash, it topples squarely into the middle of my front yard. With a feeling of satisfaction, I stand over the fallen tree. I'll bet Paul Bunyan had this feeling a lot.

On the other hand, I'll bet Mrs. Bunyan didn't spend the rest of the day crabbing about how the tree wiped out a lamp-post, bent a mailbox, and gouged up two thirds of the lawn that they had spent $200 to have chemically treated the week before.

Fortunately, winter soon will be here, and I no longer will be expected to dig holes and cut down trees. Unfortunately, spring will follow winter.

Spring is the season of love, the time of new hope and fresh beginnings. Tiny crocuses will make dots of cheerfulness in a gray world. Regal tulips will raise their glorious heads in anticipation of colorful rebirth.

Just beneath the surface of the good, rich earth, the dormant grass will awaken from its winter-long respite and begin to stretch upward in search of warming sun and nourishing sustenance.

Strengthened by the sunshine, which is free, and the nourishing sustenance, which costs $39.95 per 10,000 square feet, the grass will grow thick and high. It will cover the brown earth. It will give haven to tiny little worms that will cost $49.95 to wipe out. It will hide the nasty stuff deposited all winter by the neighbor's dog. On a warm and quiet spring morning, we will walk out into the yard, and we will find the nasty stuff left behind by the neighbor's dog. We will be barefoot.

Soon it will be time to cut the grass that has grown thick and high. We will take our lawn mower out of the garage and fill it with gasoline that costs $1.34.9 a gallon, and we will pull on the Easy-Spin starter. One hundred and forty times.

We will load the lawn mower into the backseat of the car. The gas that costs $1.34.9 a gallon will spill on the upholstery. We will drive to the lawn mower repair store. It will be closed. Come back Monday.

We will drive to church on Sunday morning with the lawn mower in the backseat. People in church will notice us. We will be the family that smells of gasoline fumes.

On Monday we will drive back to the repair store, where we will wait for an hour while the man talks on the telephone to his girlfriend. When he is finished, he will take our address and phone number. We will wonder why he takes our phone number. He never calls us when the job is finished.

After a few weeks, there will be a knock on our front door. It will be a committee of our neighbors. They will be holding a petition declaring our front yard to be an eyesore, a health hazard, and a detriment to property values. They will threaten legal action if we don't cut the grass. We will point out that if they don't stop threatening us, we will be forced to contact our lawyer. They will point out that our lawyer's name is on the petition.

We will hire a neighborhood youngster to come and cut our grass. At least we will be giving an eager young tyke the chance to make a few bucks. The eager young tyke will charge us ten bucks an hour, plus fuel charges, equipment depreciation, travel expenses, and mandatory employer contributions to his comprehensive medical and dental insurance program.

The kid will do a thorough job. He will mow every bit of grass. Not to mention the sixty feet of privet hedge we planted last fall, the two dozen tomato sets we put out last week, the tiny crocuses with their small dots of cheerfulness, and the glorious heads of the regal tulips.

Sometime in August, we will return to the lawn mower shop. The man behind the counter will add up the charges. He will use a UNIVAC 1200 Z computer. He will hand us the bill. We will feel sharp pains in our chest.

On the following Saturday, we will start the lawn mower and push it into the thick, high grass. It will hit something. It will be the eleven-year-old's aluminum baseball bat. The lawn mower will stop. We will pull on the Easy-Spin starter. One hundred and forty times. On the one hundred and forty-first time, we will hear a loud noise. It will be our back popping out. We will shuffle into the house like the Hunchback of Notre Dame.

Spring brings us many things. It brings us knee-high grass. Little worms. A lawn mower that is broken. A pain in the back. Flowers with no heads. Repair bills with no end. Nasty dog stuff on our shoes.

Spring stinks.

And I'm not too crazy about the other seasons, either.

# 10

## ONE MORE FOR THE ROAD

For a long time I thought it was pretty smart of us to have three sons and only one daughter.

Sure, boys make more noise, create more dirt, and burn out more refrigerator light bulbs. But they don't buy clothes.

Our daughter spent so much time in the department store changing room that eventually she began listing it as her home address. Every time there was a dance at her school, we had to buy her a new dress. Every time there was a dance at someone else's school, we had to buy her a new dress. Every time there was a dance anywhere in the continental United States, we had to buy her a new dress. By the time she was seventeen, she had a closet that resembled the MGM wardrobe department.

Our sons, on the other hand, never seemed to care much about clothes. A pair of Levis every few years, a new sweatshirt every few months, a pair of tennis shoes every few weeks, and they were happy.

But then our oldest boy becomes a teenager and discovers that clothes are not just something to cover his bedroom floor with. Slowly, his closet begins to fill up with clothes. And most of them are mine.

It starts gradually. A T-shirt would be missing from my dresser drawer. A hanky would go AWOL for a couple of days. A jogging suit would find its way back to my closet with strange sweat stains on it. But it really doesn't bother me until the day an entire suit of my clothes walks out the front door and I'm not in it.

"This is really getting out of control," I declare to the woman who promised to love, honor, and iron my ties. "Every-time I look, that kid is wearing my clothes."

"Count your blessings," she says, "he could be wearing my clothes."

"It's easy for you to make jokes. When the eighteen-year-old moved out, you got most of your sweaters back. But do you realize it's been almost two years since I've had the opportunity to make my own holes in my socks?"

"I really don't see what you're getting so worked up about. I seem to remember a time when you used to think it was cute when he tried on your clothes. Remember all those snapshots you took of him clomping around the house in your shoes?"

"That was a long time ago. Now I'm the one who clomps around in my shoes. He borrowed a pair of my 10½s last month, and by the time I got them back, they were 12s."

"His feet are rather large," she admits.

"Sasquatch's feet are rather large. That kid's feet are too big to parallel park. Anyway, I don't understand why he has to wear my shoes. I thought you took him to buy some a few weeks ago."

"I did."

"Don't tell me he's outgrown them in just two weeks."

"Are you kidding? He outgrew them while we were stand-ing in the checkout line. But I really think you're making too big of an issue out of this thing. So he stretches out your shoes a little bit. It's not that important."

"Maybe not. But look at this shirt he borrowed. I pay

twenty-five dollars for a Dior shirt, and when I get it back again there's a taco sauce stain on the front of it."

"I don't see what you're complaining about. It's right on top of the spaghetti sauce stain you put on it."

It's obvious that I'm not going to get much sympathy from a woman who no longer has to keep her pantyhose in a safe deposit box. But at least the kid and I have managed to work out an agreement. I get to wear my blue blazer as long as I make a reservation in writing at least five days in advance; I can wear my socks any time I can find them; and I get visitation rights with my Dex every other weekend.

And any time I want to take his mother out for dinner, I am welcome to borrow his Def Leppard T-shirt.

But the fact that he is growing bigger doesn't bother me. It's just that I seem to be growing shorter.

Half a dozen years ago, I was six-feet tall, and I spent a lot of time playing driveway basketball with him and his little friends. It was me against them. I was Kareem Abdul-Jabbar and they were the Boston Celtics, and we played until someone got called home for lunch or until the garage light got broken again.

When he hits thirteen, he seems to lose interest in driveway basketball. But one day when he is fifteen he comes into the house and says that he and some of his friends are getting up a game and they need one more player to make the sides even. So I dig my basketball shoes out of the back of the closet, locate my orthopedic sweat socks, and head for the driveway.

My fast break is interrupted by the woman who promised to love, honor, and double my dribble.

"Where are you going?" she asks.

"I'm going out to shoot a few hoops with the fifteen-year-old and his friends in the driveway."

"What about the bathroom?"

"It's not big enough. Every time you tried a hook shot your arm would get caught in the shower curtain and . . ."

"Cut that out. You know very well what I mean. For two

weeks the pipe under the downstairs bathroom sink has been leaking and you promised you'd fix it as soon as you had time."

"Well, yeah, but the other kids are waiting for me. Besides, I can fix it afterwards."

"If you go out and try to run around with those kids at your age, there may not be an afterwards."

"What do you mean, at my age? I may not be a teenager anymore, but I can still teach them a thing or two on the basketball court. I'd say I'm every bit the man I once was."

"A few more pounds and I'd say you'll be twice the man you once were."

I dribble past her and go out into the driveway, where the fifteen-year-old and four of his friends are practicing slam dunks. They look like the Harlem Globetrotters' suburban unit. One of them flips me the ball. I take a practice shot from fifteen feet. It goes thirteen feet. It's good to know that I haven't lost my shooting eye.

"What kind of a shot was that, anyway?" one of them asks.

"A jump shot."

"I thought both feet were supposed to leave the ground at the same time when you shoot a jump shot."

"I like to work up to it one foot at a time."

Sides are chosen, three to a side. I am snapped up in the sixth round. Our team huddles at the end of the driveway.

"I'll play under the basket," our team captain tells me. "And you play outside. It's safer there."

"Don't worry about me," I say, staring him straight in the belt buckle. "I can take care of myself."

The game begins and the strategy unfolds. The other team's strategy is to play patiently, work the ball inside for the good shots, and keep the ball away from us. Our team's strategy is to control the backboards, drive the lane, and keep the ball away from me.

But, eventually, the ball winds up in my hands. Quickly, I square my shoulders, bring the ball back behind my head, and shoot. At the instant I release the ball, a large shadow looms between me and the basket. It is either an opposing player or an eclipse of the sun. The ball bounces off my shoulder and goes out of bounds.

"Lucky block," I mutter, as I retrieve the ball from the neighbor's yard.

Several minutes later I get the ball again and try another shot. This time it is different. This time the ball winds up three neighbors' yards away. I retrieve it and bring it back.

By the end of the game I have attempted nine shots and seen more of the neighborhood than I have in the past six months. But we win 88-74, with the help of my four points. Not to mention my rebound.

After his friends have left, the fifteen-year-old thanks me for playing and mentions that anytime I feel like playing again I should let him know.

"Really?" I say.

"Sure," he says. "Just get some of your little friends together and I'll be glad to take you on."

On days that I come home from work and find that our driveway is not filled with teenage boys, I know that there can be only one reason. It is because they all are in our basement.

"I'm not sure what makes our house the neighborhood youth center. According to the resident fifteen-year-old, not only is ours the only house in the free world without a VCR attached to a giant screen, he has been a social outcast ever since it was learned that he is the only fifteen-year-old in the whole school without a car, a moped, a snowmobile, a telephone, a $75 class ring, a $150-a-week allowance, and a 5 A.M. curfew.

And yet, for some reason, our house constantly is overrun with teenage boys. It really hits me one evening when I come home from work and find a line of them backed up out the front door. I manage to find a parking spot within walking distance of the house, park the car, walk to my yard, and elbow my way through the crowd. Just inside the foyer, a teenager the size of Merlin Olsen grabs my arm.

"Hey," he growls, "stand in line."

"It's OK," I say, "I'm a friend of the manager."

Inside, I manage to locate the woman who promised to love, honor, and save me a reservation.

"Can I ask you something personal?" I inquire.

"Sure."

"I was just wondering. About how many teenagers would you say we have. I don't need an exact count right now. A ballpark figure will do."

"Well, there's the eighteen-year-old, but I'm pretty sure she moved out to her own place a few months ago. At least, it's been that long since any of my skirts have been missing. And then, we also have a fifteen-year-old."

"Any others?"

"I don't think so. Why?"

"Oh, nothing special. I was just curious about who all these boys are when I come home from work every day."

"There do seem to be quite a few of them," she admits.

"Quite a few? I've seen video game arcades that didn't have this many teenage boys in it. I think I'll go down to the basement and find out what they're all doing here."

In the basement I find four kids shooting pool, several sitting around the stereo leafing through albums, and the rest just sort of lounging around. I don't recognize most of them, although one kid stretched out on the floor does look sort of familiar. Come to think of it, every time I've ever seen him at our house he's been stretched out on the floor. I think they wheel him in that way.

My entrance into the basement is not exactly a scene from "Father Knows Best." When Jim Anderson came into a room, the three teenagers who had been sitting at attention on the couch would jump to their feet, adjust their ties, and say in unison, "Gosh, Mr. Anderson, it's nice to see you again. Bud has been letting us look at your keen collection of Glenn Miller albums. They're real groovy."

When I walk into the basement, two kids belch, one streaks a nine-inch chalk mark on my pool table, and one heads for the bathroom. The rest ignore me completely. On the couch, two kids are looking at my collection of Barry Manilow albums.

"What a pud," one says. I think that means "keen."

"Uh, excuse me," I say, finally, "has anyone seen Mike?"

"Who?" asks a kid who is standing in the corner with the refrigerator under his arm.

"Mike. He's the kid who lives here."

"What's he look like?"

"Reddish hair, about five foot eleven, size nineteen Nike's."

"Naw. I've been here every day and I haven't seen him in a couple of weeks."

At that moment, a public service announcement they used to run on television flashes through my mind.

"It's nine o'clock," the announcement began. "Do you know where your kids are?"

OK, so maybe I don't always know where my teenager is. But I'll bet I know where *Yours* is.

When you have teenage boys hanging around in your basement, I suppose nothing you hear from down there really should surprise you. Still, I am stunned one quiet evening as we are sitting in the living room and suddenly an electronic screeching noise erupts from downstairs.

"Ohmygod," I shout, jumping up from my chair, "the water softener has exploded. Head for the exits. Fathers and children first. Don't panic. No shoving."

"Relax," says the woman who promised to love, honor, and paddle my lifeboat, "it's not the water softener. It's the fifteen-year-old."

"The fifteen-year-old has exploded?"

"The fifteen-year-old is playing his guitar."

"Oh, thank goodness," I sigh, dropping back into my chair. "For a minute there I thought we were goners. It's certainly a relief to . . . guitar? What guitar?"

"The one he got a couple of weeks ago while you were out of town on your business trip."

"Why didn't you tell me?"

"I've been waiting for the right moment. You don't always handle news like this very well."

"What's that supposed to mean?"

"Remember how you carried on when I called you at work and told you we thought the dog was pregnant?"

"Of course I carried on. I warned you that we should have enrolled her in that sex education class. But this is different. Putting a guitar in the hands of a fifteen-year-old is like slipping Norman Bates a butcher knife. I can't believe you let him bring one of those things into our house."

"I don't see why you're so upset. I'd think you'd be happy that he's continuing his interest in music."

"Who's talking about music? I'm talking about the noise that comes out of those guitars. What kids today call music isn't exactly the kind of stuff that would make Beethoven wish he had his hearing back."

"You know, you're starting to sound like a real old fogey," she says. "I think kids today have very well developed musical tastes."

"Oh really? Apparently you've already forgotten the last teenage party we had here. The one where the smoke alarm went off and six of them got up and danced."

"Well, if you've got a problem with him playing the guitar, I suggest that you go down and talk to him about it."

"I'm going to do just that."

I walk downstairs and fight my way through the sound waves to his room. Judging by the noise, not only has he found the lost chord, he is giving it the thrashing of its life. When I open the door, I find him sitting on the floor in the middle of his room. There is a guitar on his lap and enough electrical equipment around him to brown out the eastern United States. He does not hear me when I walk in. I am not surprised. With all the noise coming out of his speakers, he would not hear the Mormon Tabernacle Choir if it walked in.

I reach down and pull out his plug.

"Oh, hi," he says. "What's up?"

"Probably our electric bill, for one," I say. "About this guitar."

"Great, isn't it? As soon as I learn how to play it a little better, maybe I'll join a rock band. So far I've only had two lessons."

"With two lessons you're probably overqualified for about half the rock bands in the country," I point out. "Anyway, I don't see why you need all this equipment."

"It's really not much. Just a couple of speakers and an amplifier."

"Radio Free Europe operates with less equipment than this."

"Boy, I'll bet Elmer Presley's father didn't give him this much flak when he was learning to play guitar."

"That's Elvis. Besides, he didn't actually play his guitar. It was just something to hold onto to keep him from undulating himself off the edge of the stage."

"I don't know anything about that. All I know is that I'm going to keep practicing and maybe someday I'll be in a real famous rock band."

I stop and think about that. My kid in a rock band. Traveling around the country with tons of equipment and dozens of roadies. Playing at sold-out rock concerts. Making millions of dollars. Buying his dad a house in Beverly Hills. It's the least he can do for the man who provided the encouragement to help launch his career.

But wearing my clothes and getting into rock music are just two of the major indicators that tell us he is growing up. There is one more way we can tell, and the signs are as obvious as a single zit.

The same shopping center that was "just around the corner" when he was fourteen and wanted to go there with his buddies to feed quarters into electronic games now is "way too far to walk." The girl for whom he would have climbed the highest mountain six months ago now lives "in another country, practically."

He is fifteen years old, and the campaign for a car has begun.

It is a low-key campaign at first, filled with soft sighs when we drive him past a used-car lot, wistful looks when a teenager's car cruises past the house. Soon he progresses to making sounds like a '63 Chevy at the dinner table. Instead of lounging around in his room throwing imaginary touchdown passes to make-believe receivers, he is sitting at his desk and downshifting from third to second. Before we know it, he is salivating whenever he hears the jingle of car keys.

Then he starts to get serious. Every conversation is fuel-injected. Every action is done in four-wheel drive. The closer he gets to sixteen, the more intense and single-minded the campaign becomes. One afternoon I greet him when he comes home from school.

"How was school?" I ask.

"Fine. The parking lot was really crowded."

"That's nice. What's happening with the basketball team?"

"Nothing much. The center has a broken clutch plate and one of the guards needs a ring job."

"Sorry to hear that. By the way, don't forget that the Browns are on TV next Sunday. It should be a great game."

"Yeah, I don't want to miss that. That's the one being sponsored by Lincoln-Mercury."

"That reminds me, I've been meaning to ask you something. Have you been looking at my *Playboy*? Somebody took it out of my desk without asking."

"What makes you think it was me?"

"The Datsun ads were all wrinkled."

"Yeah, it was me. If you think I should be punished, go ahead and ground me. Even if I could go out, I don't have any way to get to places."

"Is there something you're trying to tell me?"

"Well, seeing as how you brought it up, I was wondering how long it was going to be before I get a car."

"What's the rush? You're only fifteen."

"Fifteen and a half. And if we don't start looking for a car pretty quick, all the good ones will be gone by the time I'm sixteen."

"I read the papers pretty closely, but I don't remember reading anything about a used-car shortage. Besides, what makes you think you're getting a car when you're sixteen?"

"I just assumed I was. Everybody in school has one."

"I'm sure that not everybody in school has a car. I went past your school the other day and saw lots of people getting off public buses."

"Yeah, but those were teachers. Every kid over sixteen drives his own car to school."

Life hasn't been easy for him. He was the only kid in elementary school who didn't have a BMX. He was the only kid in junior high who didn't have a moped. Soon he'll be the only kid in high school who doesn't have a car.

And I don't have the heart to tell him that things won't necessarily get any better when he grows up. I, for instance, am the only husband on the block who does not have a twenty-one-foot Evinrude with twin inboard engines.

I spend the next six months trying to steer conversations away from cars, but, inevitably, the day arrives that I no longer can dodge the question.

I remember that day perfectly. Veronica Hamel is leaning close to me, a lock of long brown hair brushing against her fashionably high cheekbone. She is murmuring the reasons why she is tired of flat-bellied Italian police captains and would really prefer a slightly rounded middle-aged columnist. They all are good reasons. Just as she is getting to number seven, the one about the feeling she gets in the pit of her stomach when she comes near a man with ink on his fingers, a hand seizes my shoulder and shakes me.

I open my eyes and try to focus them in the dim light of the bedroom. There is someone standing over me. It is not Veronica Hamel. It is not even Ed Marinaro. It is my oldest son.

"Hey, Dad," he shouts, "let's go get my temps."

"Your what?" I mumble, groggily.

"My temps. You know, my temporary driver's license. I'm sixteen today."

"Happy birthday. What time is it?"

"About 6:30."

"A.M.?"

"Of course. C'mon, let's go."

"Take it easy. The people at the license bureau aren't at work this early. There probably are roosters who aren't at work this early. Besides, I think the car keys are in my other pajamas."

At breakfast, I mention to the woman who promised to love, honor, and scramble my bacon that the sixteen-year-old seems fairly interested in getting his temporary driver's license today.

"That probably explains why he slept on the hood of the station wagon last night," she says. "I suppose you might as well take him and get it over with."

"Isn't there some kind of a written test he has to pass first?"

"Don't worry about that. He's been studying the manual every night for a month. He's memorized every word, including the introduction, the location of every license bureau in the state, and the address of the company that printed the booklet."

"Is this the same kid who has to have his phone number written in ink on the toes of his tennis shoes?"

"I didn't think it was possible, either," she admits. "But if they gave the SATs on the Ohio Highway Code, this kid would have a four-year scholarship tomorrow."

I finish breakfast and drive the sixteen-year-old to the license bureau. We fill out some papers, then he goes into another room to take his tests. The kid who hasn't heard his mother calling him for dinner since he was eight years old gets a perfect score on the hearing test. The kid who drove the rider mower through two dozen staked tomato plants because he "didn't see them," breezes through two eye examinations. The kid who had trouble with American history because he couldn't remember who the British fought in the Revolutionary War scores 100 on the written questions.

Then the clerk gives him his temporary driver's license, and he is sprinting out to the parking lot with my car keys in his hand. By the time I get to the parking lot, he is behind the wheel, with the radio on and the key in the ignition.

"Wait a minute," I say. "Just because you have your temps doesn't mean you know how to drive. Learning to operate a car with a stick shift like this one takes some experience."

"Hey, don't worry, Dad, I've been driving my buddies' cars for a year. I know all about these things."

To prove it, he starts the car, steps on the gas, and starts out of the parking lot. When he reaches third gear, he decides to try the clutch. As we head toward the street, several highway patrolmen turn to watch us. I'm not surprised. It's probably not every day that they see a car pop a wheelie in their parking lot. Or a grown man sobbing.

But, for the sixteen-year-old, the day for which he had waited a lifetime is bittersweet.

That evening there is a family party, with cake and ice cream and candles and singing that is just a little bit off-key. And then it is time to open his presents, a small stack of them, with an envelope on top.

"I'll save this one for last," he says, smiling and putting the envelope to one side. He starts with the smallest package and works his way up: tube socks from his little brothers, a shirt from his big sister, a tennis racquet from his parents.

Then he picks up the envelope, anticipation clear on his face. He likes to save the best for last, and the look of anticipation grows as he opens the envelope, takes out the typed card inside. Reads it.

It is an invitation from his dad for dinner at the finest

restaurant in town, the same invitation his big sister received when she turned sixteen, the same invitation his little brothers will receive when they are sixteen. It's important, their dad feels, for someone of sixteen to be acquainted with the experience of dining at a place where the food is not wrapped in cardboard and dessert is not served with a plastic spoon by someone chewing gum. He does not want them to grow up and get married and walk into a fine restaurant on their wedding night and have the waiter open a bottle of champagne and pour a little into the glass and be embarrassed because the waiter has to tell them what to do next, the way a waiter had to tell their dad.

He reads the card again, and the look of anticipation on his face dies.

"Thanks," he says, quietly, putting aside the invitation and taking a small bite of birthday cake. He keeps his face down, looking at nothing in particular. But the disappointment is clear.

He had hoped for a car.

We had tried to convince him that there would not be a car on his sixteenth birthday, that even though he is old enough to drive now, that even though many of his buddies have cars, there would not be one for him.

"That's all right," he had said. "I don't expect one."

But he did, really. His dad liked to surprise him like that. When he was twelve and the only thing he wanted for Christmas was a ten-speed bike, he came downstairs early in the morning and looked at all the presents under the tree. But none of the boxes with his name on it was anywhere near big enough to have a bike inside. He opened them one at a time, from the smallest to the largest, thanking his little brothers for the tube socks, thanking his big sister for the shirt, thanking his parents for whatever it was they gave him that year.

When all the presents were opened and he was fighting against the tears, his dad said to him. "How about bringing in a couple of logs for the fireplace?"

So he opened the garage door and there it was, a shiny new ten-speed with all the gears and just the right kind of pedals. And he threw his arms around his dad, hugging him as hard as he could, and then it was his dad's turn to fight against the tears.

He thought maybe it was going to be that way this time, that inside the envelope there would be something about a car. And his dad would have liked for it to be that way. It had been a long time since that hug. It was tempting to buy another one.

At his sixteenth birthday party, his dad wants to explain to him why it is different this time, why there is no shiny car waiting in the garage. He wants to explain that a car is not the same as a bike. It is not just a way to get to school, not just something with which to impress girls, not merely a status symbol to help you keep up with your buddies.

In our society, a car is a means of leaving childhood, a vehicle that takes you into adulthood. A symbol of maturity. But you can't buy maturity for your child. You can't go to a used-car lot and make a down payment on adulthood for someone else. It is one of those things for which you have to get up early on a summer morning and cut lawns and carry grocery bags and sweep floors and walk past the video games without spending any of the money that you have saved.

His dad would like to say all that, but he is not sure that this is the right time, so he doesn't say anything. He only hopes that some day his son will know that the reason there is no car on his sixteenth birthday is not because his parents do not love him. But because they do.

It takes him a few days, but finally he recovers from the disappointment of not getting a car for his birthday. I know he is recovered, because when I walk into the living room he doesn't snarl at me. In fact, he smiles. He speaks.

"Need anything from the store?" he asks.

"No thanks," I reply. "Mom just went shopping this morning."

"I could drive over and pick up the laundry."

"They deliver."

"Need anything taken to the bank?"

"Nope."

"How about if I cruise out to the end of the driveway and check the mail?"

"The mailman hasn't been here yet."

"I could drive around and look for him."

"Look," I say, "I know you're eager to start driving. But before you take the car out of the garage, we've got to make arrangements for insurance."

"I'll drive over and take care of it."

"Never mind. I'll phone."

I call our insurance agent and tell him that I have a sixteen-year-old boy who just got his driver's license. The phone goes dead in my ear. Obviously an equipment malfunction. I call back. His secretary answers this time. She tells me our insurance agent has just left on vacation.

"When will he be back?" I ask.

"When will your sixteen-year-old be twenty-five?" she asks.

"Are you trying to tell me that he's reluctant to insure our sixteen-year-old?"

"Let me put it this way," she says. "As an insurance risk, a sixteen-year-old boy driving ranks somewhere between Evel Knievel and Stevie Wonder."

I try five other insurance companies before I find one willing to cover him. Not only do they insure him, they offer a reduced rate based upon academic achievement and citizenship. Which could be a real break for me. Assuming, of course, that within the next three months the sixteen-year-old graduates magna cum laude from Harvard and wins the Congressional Medal of Honor.

With his insurance taken care of, the sixteen-year-old steps up his campaign to drive the car. He offers to pick up his little brothers after soccer practice. He insists that he needs the car to go to school because the bus takes too long and he can't wait to get there. He asks for the car keys to drive the garbage cans to the curb.

Finally, one evening after dinner he announces that if he is not at the library in the next fifteen minutes to get a book on American history, he probably will fail the course and possibly be deported.

"I'm awfully busy right now," I say, "can't your mother take you?"

"She's busy, too. Looks like I'm going to be forced to drive."

I think about that. I'm still not convinced that he's ready to drive alone. On the other hand, if I don't show some confidence in him soon, he might begin to doubt himself and not grow into the self-assured adult we want him to become. A show of confidence at this point could be crucial to his development. I'm just going to have to suck in my breath and take a chance.

"OK," I say. "Take your mother's car."

He grabs the keys and sprints to the garage.

"Where's he going so fast?" asks the woman who promised to love, honor, and call the tow truck as he breezes past her.

"He has to go to the library. I told him he could take your car."

"You did *what*?"

"I told him he could take your car. After all, he's a licensed driver who has reached a point in his life of sufficient maturity to assume the responsibilities and obligations of adulthood."

"If he's so mature, why don't you let him take your car?"

"Are you out of your mind? Do you think I'm going to give the keys to a sports car to a kid who can't push a vacuum cleaner through the living room without totaling the couch?"

While the sixteen-year-old is gone with the car, we drink four pots of coffee and smoke seven packs of cigarettes. It is the longest twenty minutes of our lives. But eventually he returns and pulls the car into the garage, unscratched. He strolls into the house, tosses the keys on the table, and heads for his room.

"Any problems?" I ask.

"Of course not," he says.

"Good. Were you able to get your book checked out before the library closed?"

"Book?" he asks.

From then on, every time he smiles, I get nervous. It gets so that the sight of his teeth gives me heart palpitations. So I am braced for the worst on the day he does three cartwheels into the dining room, kisses his little brother, flashes an eighty−eight−tooth smile at me and asks, "Hey, Dad, are you doing anything special after dinner?"

"Why?" I hedge, my suspicions increasing.

"I was hoping you'd go with me to check out a car I saw for sale."

"A car? What are you going to do with a car?"

"I could drive it to work."

"You don't have a job," I point out.

"That's because I don't have a car to get there," he points out. Living with a teenager is an endless round of Catch−22s.

After dinner we drive to a used−car lot, and he directs me to an area that obviously is the Baltic Avenue section of the board. A dozen or so vehicles are standing around, hanging their fenders in shame. All of them have seen better days. But not recently. They are the kind of cars a junkyard dog would help you steal.

"Boy, I really didn't think you'd agree to come with me, tonight," the sixteen−year−old says as we get out of our car. "Thanks a lot."

"Think nothing of it," I say. "Besides, I always wondered what Jim Rockford did with his cars when he was finished with them."

We pick our way through the lot until we come to the car he wants to show me. It is a 1974 Toyota with four good tires, 80,000 miles on the odometer, and a coat of white paint that appears to have been applied recently. With a roller. At midnight.

"What do you think?" the sixteen−year−old asks.

"It has a certain, uh, distinctiveness to it," I concede. What else can you say about a car that has a reflector dangling from the side of its fender, ventilated rocker panels, and an interior that appears to have been customized by the IRA?

A salesman approches us.

"Can I help you folks today?" he asks.

"I'd say this car needs help more than we do," I say.

"It could use a little work," he admits. When a salesman says a car "could use a little work," he means there's nothing wrong with it that can't be taken care of with a little bit of effort, a few tools, and a magic wand.

The salesman unlocks the car so we can get a better look at the inside. The sixteen-year-old immediately slides in behind the wheel and turns on the radio. I think it's a conditioned response.

"Would you like to take it for a little drive?" the salesman asks.

"Will you be coming along?"

"Well, actually, I'm awfully busy right now," he says. He hands the keys to the sixteen-year-old and quickly steps back ten paces. The sixteen-year-old inserts the key and turns it. The car comes to life instantly. With a blast of noise from the muffler that shatters the rear-view mirror.

"IT HAS A REAL RESONANCE, DOESN'T IT?" the salesman shouts.

"WORLD WAR II HAD RESONANCE," I shout back. "THIS THING COULD DROWN OUT THE INDY 500."

The sixteen-year-old shifts into gear and takes his foot off the brake. The engine dies before he can get his foot to the gas pedal.

"How come it quit when I took my foot off the brake?" he asks. "Do you think there's something wrong with the engine."

"Not necessarily," I say. "It might just be a safety feature."

He starts the car again, with his foot on the gas pedal. We pull out of the lot. On the fly.

"I WONDER IF THE HORN WORKS," the sixteen-year-old shouts.

"THE LAST THING THIS CAR NEEDS IS A HORN," I shout back. "HOW DOES IT HANDLE."

"IT PULLS A LITTLE BIT TO THE RIGHT."

"I WONDERED WHY WE WERE GOING AROUND IN A CIRCLE."

Twenty minutes later, we pull back into the lot, he takes his foot off the gas pedal, and the engine dies.

"Well," says the salesman, "what do you think?"

"SAY WHAT?" I shout.

"I love it," the sixteen-year-old says.

"I can write it up for you right now," the salesman offers.

"We'll think about it," I say, dragging the sixteen-year-old back to our car.

For the next two days, the sixteen-year-old can talk of nothing else but that car.

"If you let me get it, I'll do anything I have to do to pay for it," he vows. "I'll dig ditches. I'll pick cotton. I'll work eighteen hours a day in a filthy coal mine until my little lungs turn black and my young body is wracked with coughs and I start spitting up . . ."

"Put a lid on it, Camille," I interrupt. "Before we make a decision about buying that car, I think we should have it checked out. I'm not sure it's worth the money."

"Dad, that car's beautiful."

"That car looks like third runner-up in the demolition derby. But that's not what's worrying me. I'm more concerned about the way it runs. If we're seriously thinking about buying it, I think we should take it and go see a reputable mechanic."

"Whatever you think is fine with me," says the sixteen-year-old. "I'll do anything I have to."

"All right, then, tomorrow come straight home from school and drive it over to my mechanic to have him check it out."

"Tomorrow? Tomorrow's my guitar lesson. I can't miss that. Can't somebody else drive it over there?"

"Remind me never to hire you to work in my coal mine."

The next day I take the afternoon off, drive to the used-car lot, and tell the salesman that I'd like to take the car to my mechanic to be checked.

"Is it far from here?" the salesman asks.

"About five miles. Is that too far?"

"Not if it's all downhill."

He hands me the keys and mentions that they've done some work on it since we test drove it the other day.

"I noticed that when you took your foot off the gas pedal it stalled a few times," he explains. "So I had our repairman turn up the idle a bit. That should take care of the problem."

I thank him, start the car, and drive out of the lot. Turning up the idle has not toned down the muffler, which still is loud enough to drown out a rock concert. But at least the car does not stop when I take my foot off the gas pedal. Not only does it not stop when I take my foot off the gas pedal, it barely slows down when I step on the brake. When I come to the first intersection, I have to put both feet on the brake pedal to keep it from idling through a red light. It is the first car I ever have driven that has more power in idle than it has in passing gear.

I drive to my mechanic's garage. As I pull into the service area, he sees me. He looks at the car I am driving. He appears to be amused. Of course, I could be imagining that. It's just that never before have I seen a mechanic drop $200 worth of tools, fall ten feet from a hydraulic lift, and roll around on a garage floor clutching his stomach and laughing hysterically.

"What's that?" he asks when finally he was wiped away the last of his tears.

"It's a car my son is thinking of buying," I inform him. "I want to see if you can fix it up without too much expense."

"Hey, man, I'm your mechanic, not your fairy godmother."

"Certainly with all the equipment you have around here, you ought to be able to do something with it."

"Not unless there's a ticket to Lourdes in the bottom of my

tool box," he says. "But I'll check it out anyway, if it'll make you feel better."

He opens the hood, pokes around the engine for a while, and then attaches a gadget to the block.

"What's that for?" I ask.

"It's to check the compression," he says, looking at a gauge at the end of the gadget and shaking his head like a doctor who has just diagnosed bubonic plague.

"Something wrong?" I ask.

"It barely reaches 100," he says.

"Is that bad?"

"Let me put it this way. If this car was a person, right now I'd be putting my arm around your shoulders and suggesting that you start looking for headstones."

I thank him for his advice and drive the car back to the lot. The sixteen-year-old is going to be disappointed when he hears the news. Especially after he worked so hard for this car.

To tell the truth, I am not all that upset that the clunker at the used-car lot didn't work out. I have always felt at a disadvantage when dealing with used-car salesmen. In fact, when used-car salesmen pray, I'm the guy they pray for. When it comes time to buy a used car, I have just enough mechancial aptitude to walk around the car once or twice, say "hmmm" a few times, and kick a tire. If nothing falls off, I figure the car probably is better than the one I drove in with.

In fifteen years of tire-kicking, I accumulated a '56 Chevy that dropped a transmission in my driveway, a '63 Falcon that threw a rod on the freeway, and three broken toes.

All of which makes me feel a little bit more confident when the sixteen-year-old says he has heard of a used car being sold by a private owner in our neighborhood.

We drive over to see the car, which is parked in a driveway a few miles from our house. As we pull into the driveway, a white-haired gentleman in overalls comes out of the house. He looks as if he has just escaped from a Grant Wood painting. If I look in his living room, I suspect, I will find a white-haired woman holding his pitchfork. Immediately, I feel reassured. I'd much rather deal with a man like this than some high–pressure, fast–talking, used–car salesman in a flashy sport coat.

"Howdy, neighbor," I say. "My boy here is interested in buying your car."

"Well, sir, he could do a lot worse than this little baby. Yes, indeed, friend, I'm amazed that this bargain has lasted as long as it has. It's a real low–mileage cream puff. Matter of fact, if I only had more room in my garage, I'd keep it for myself. They don't make 'em like this no more. Better snap it up while you've got the chance, good buddy, because I've got three other buyers just dying to get their hands on it."

Suddenly, I get the feeling that if I look in Farmer Brown's closet, I will find 17 flashy sport coats. And a diploma from the K–Tel School of Speed Talking.

"I wonder if I could take it for a little test drive?" I ask.

"Don't see why not, friend," he says. "Drive it clean around the block if you want to. Course, I'll have to ask you not to get it up over thirty miles an hour. Insurance. You understand."

"Oh. Right."

I back the car out of the driveway, coast down the street, and pull around the corner. When I am out of view, I push the gas pedal to the floor. His insurance company has nothing to worry about. This car wouldn't reach thirty miles an hour if it fell over a cliff.

I drive back to the house.

"Great little car, isn't it?" Farmer Brown says.

"Seems a little sluggish."

"Probably got some bad gas."

"Probably," I agree. "Can I take a look at the engine?"

"Go right ahead."

I pop open the hood. A cloud of smoke billows out. It is like putting your head inside Mount St. Helens.

"Seems to be a little smoke coming out of the engine," I point out when the oxygen has returned to my lungs.

"Where? I don't see any smoke," Farmer Brown says.

"That's probably because you've got that wet cloth over your face. There was less smoke than this inside the *Hindenberg*."

"Oh, *that* smoke. Well, I wouldn't worry about that. It's my cat. That rascal likes to crawl up under the hood when the car is parked, and a lot of his fur gets stuck in there and burns when the engine gets hot. That's all it is."

When the last of the smoke finally drifts away, I put my head back down into the engine compartment and look around. Not only is his cat losing his fur, he's leaking oil.

"What are you looking for, Dad?" the sixteen-year-old asks, putting his head under the hood with mine. "Engine wear?"

"Kitty litter."

Despite my reservations, I write out a check for Farmer Brown, and the sixteen-year-old drives home with his first car. Two days later he calls me from work.

"Can you come and pick me up, Dad? My car won't start."

I knew I should have kicked the tires. Not to mention Farmer Brown. And Mrs. Brown. And their bald cat.

# 11

## THE EGGS
## AND I

There are all sorts of child-raising books on the market.

There are books on how to raise healthy children. Books on how to raise happy children. Book on how to raise healthy, happy children. Books on how to raise healthy, happy, creative, well-adjusted children who will grow up to be honest, courteous, kind, trustworthy, and fit to move in with the Brady Bunch.

I'd settle for a book that will tell me how to get them to eat fried eggs.

I never realized how big a problem that could be until one Saturday-morning when the woman who promised to love, honor, and keep my sunny side up goes off to work, leaving behind a note about meals. For lunch, the note says, I am to feed them two eggs each.

At lunchtime I cook up a pound of sausage links, a stack of

toast, and half a dozen fried eggs. When everything is ready, I call them to the table.

The eleven-year-old arrives first.

"Oh, gross," he yells when I put his plate in front of him. "Gag me with a spoon. I think I'm gonna barf my brains out."

"Is there something that doesn't appeal to you?" I inquire.

"My eggs are staring at me."

"They are not staring at you. Those are two perfectly prepared fried eggs. I know short-order cooks who would give their left spatula to be able to make eggs like those."

"Mom always makes our eggs scrambled," he says.

"Well, Mom's not here and I happen to feel that real men don't eat scrambled eggs."

"But fried eggs are disgusting," he says, grabbing a sausage link and dipping it into the peanut butter jar. "The yellow parts bleed all over the plate when you stick your fork into them and the white parts are slimy and there's that other stuff that's sort of clear-colored and it hangs down off of your fork like . . ."

"I know what it hangs down off your fork like," I interrupt. If he keeps on like this, I'm gonna barf *my* brains out. On the other hand, it's nice to know that the art of mealtime conversation is not dead at our house.

The eleven-year-old sticks his fork into the egg white, cuts off a piece too small to be seen by the naked eye, and puts it into his mouth.

"Hey," he says, "there's something hard in my egg. It's probably a shell."

"Fried eggs are supposed to be crunchy," I inform him.

A few minutes later he is joined at the table by his brothers.

"Fried eggs," groans the eight-year-old. "Sick."

"If I want a medical opinion I'll call Marcus Welby," I tell him. "Now just sit there and eat. Your mother said you're supposed to have eggs for lunch, and that's what you're going to have. Besides, eggs are good for you."

"Why?" he demands.

"Well, they, uh, they make your coat glossy."

"Actually," chips in the sixteen-year-old, "eggs are high in cholesterol, which collects on the inner walls of arteries, resulting in arteriosclerosis, which narrows the blood vessels and deprives organs of food and oxygen." I've always felt that being a parent was tough enough without our schools wasting tax dollars teaching kids things like science.

"That may be, Christiaan Barnard," I tell the sixteen-year-old. "But you and your blood vessels are going to sit there until every last bite of egg is gone. Now start chewing."

All three of them begin to nibble around the edges of their eggs. Satisfied that I have things under control, I go into the living room to read the paper. When I return to the kitchen fifteen minutes later, all three kids are gone, their plates are cleaner than they were when I got them out of the cupboard, and the dog has a smile on her face and half a pound of egg yolk in her whiskers.

My first impulse is to go outside, drag them back to the kitchen, and cook up another batch of fried eggs for them to eat. But I decide that I'd better conserve my strength.

Her note says that I'm supposed to feed them liver for dinner.

Even though I am blessed with a kitchen full of kids who will not eat fried eggs, liver, or any other food in which the vitamins outnumber the chemicals, I enjoy cooking occasionally, especially on weekends. Mysteriously, this does not seem to overjoy the woman who promised to love, honor, and lick my platter clean. Frequently, she barely touches the meals that I spend all day preparing.

"You seem depressed," I point out after watching her pick at her dinner one Sunday. "In fact, every weekend that I cook you seem depressed. I'd think you'd be happy, considering how much work I save you by making dinner."

"Were the people of Georgia happy because General Sherman saved them all the work of having to air condition their plantations?"

"What's that supposed to mean?"

"It's supposed to mean that the Union Army didn't cause as much of a mess going from Atlanta to the sea as you do every weekend going from the refrigerator to the stove. And Mrs. Sherman didn't have to clean up after them, either."

"Mess? What mess? I always clean up after I get done in the kitchen."

"How about the grease spots you left on top of the stove yesterday?"

"OK, so maybe I missed a spot or two."

"How can you miss a spot that is two feet long? And three inches deep."

"Nobody's perfect."

"And what about the refried beans you made last weekend that splattered all over the wall? If I ever get them scraped off, we'll have enough to feed every family from here to Acapulco."

"You have to break an egg to make an omelet," I remind her.

"Maybe so. But you don't have to throw the eggshells on the floor."

"I already told you, that was an accident. Besides, I thought the dog would take care of it."

"Just our luck, we don't happen to have a dog that eats eggshells. She also doesn't happen to eat green peppers, carrots, zucchini, celery, or any of the other vegetable scraps that always wind up on the floor every time you make minestrone. I'm telling you, something is going to have to change. Agreed?"

"You're absolutely right. Let's trade in the dog and get a rabbit."

"Come on, I'm serious. I don't like to put it this way, but if we don't get this worked out pretty soon, I'm afraid there are going to have to be some drastic changes in our relationship."

"Separate bedrooms?"

"Separate kitchens."

It's not as if I am a blatant slob. But there's no pleasing the woman. She insists that I would not be comfortable living in anything cleaner than the La Brea tar pits. I, on the other hand, think that perhaps she's just a bit too fussy. Of course, I could be wrong. Maybe she's not the only woman in town who vacuums the front lawn.

Even when I don't cook, these philosophical differences cause some conflicts in the kitchen. Take, for instance, washing dishes. She feels that they have to be washed after every meal. I figure any dish that doesn't have something growing on it probably is clean enough.

Usually, she washes the dishes to her satisfaction and everything works out fine. Until the day she goes off to spend a week at her mother's, leaving me home with a full refrigerator, an empty sink, and a herd of kids who think they're headed for anorexia nervosa if they don't get to eat every half hour.

At first, it works out fairly well. After each meal I simply pile the dirty dishes in the sink. After the first day, the sink is full. After the second day, the sink is overflowing. After the third day, the eleven-year-old is standing in the middle of the kitchen, lobbing cups like hand grenades to the top of the pile.

"I think we're gonna have to wash dishes pretty soon, Dad," he says.

"Either that or get a kitchen with higher ceilings," I agree. "I guess I'll do them after dinner."

"How?"

"What do you mean, how?"

"I mean, are you going to use the automatic dishwasher?"

"No, I'm going to tie them to the top of the station wagon and drive through a car wash. Of course I'm going to use the dishwasher. Why wouldn't I?"

"Mom says the last time you tried it you didn't do such a good job."

"That's just because a few plates got melted. It could have happened to anybody. I probably didn't arrange them exactly right."

"Mom said it looked like you stood in the living room and sailed them in there like Frisbees."

"Never mind what Mom said. Find me the stepladder so I can get to the top of this pile."

After dinner I start to work. The secret of using an automatic dishwasher is proper loading. Cups and plates go in their slots on the top rack. Pots and pans go on the bottom rack. Silverware belongs in the little compartments in front.

I fill the top rack, carefully arranging the plates so that each one has its own space. I put the pots and pans on the bottom rack, making sure that each one is placed to receive maximum washing exposure. By the time the washer is full, I still have service for fifty left in the sink. At this rate, I'm going to be washing all night. Some rearranging is called for.

I put two plates in each slot. I relocate the pans so that each one gets reasonable washing exposure. When I turn back to the sink, the pile is higher than it was when I started. I am beginning to suspect that the plates on the bottom are reproducing.

I take an armful of plates off the top of the pile, jam them into the dishwasher, put my shoulder against the door, force it shut, and turn on the switch.

The dishwasher begins to hum. Satisfied, I go into the living room to watch television. A few minutes later I hear the eleven-year-old calling me from the kitchen.

"Hey, Dad, the dishwasher's making a funny noise."

"What kind of a funny noise?"

"I don't know. It sounds like somebody in there is trying to get out."

"How long has it been since you've seen the dog?"

"It's not her. She's out in the backyard."

I return to the kitchen. The dishwasher no longer is humming. It is banging, clanking, and rattling, the last time I heard noise like that, it was coming from the sixteen-year-old's stereo. I turn off the switch and open the door. Hot steam pours out into my face. Hot water pours out onto my foot. The dishes that were in the top rack have fallen onto the bottom rack. Except for the ones that are melted.

It is obvious that I have been defeated once again and that

no more dishes are going to get washed tonight. Unless, of course, I can find an all-night car wash.

Even though she doesn't like to have me in her kitchen, there's nothing that the woman who promised to love, honor, and tie my apron strings likes better than to have me cook out. It's one of those little ironies that makes our marriage so much more interesting than Jim and Margaret's.

I mean, we moved to the suburbs because we wanted to live where it was quiet, and now we are surrounded by neighbors who use power mowers with engines big enough to win the pole position at Indy. We picked a lot with half an acre of grass so the kids would have plenty of space to play, and now we have a teenager who hasn't left his room since the Ford administration and two little boys who spend every waking minute riding skateboards down the middle of the street.

And we bought a house with air conditioning, a microwave oven, and a dining room big enough to seat the Pittsburgh Steelers. And now any day there is less than six inches of snow on the patio, she wants me to cook out.

"I don't get it," I say. "What can I burn over three pounds of charcoal in the backyard that you can't burn just as well on the stove in the kitchen."

"That's not the point," she replies. "Eating outside is much more carefree. Besides, food cooked on a grill tastes so much better."

"Food cooked on a grill tastes like charcoal lighter." I point out. "I don't think a hamburger should have an octane rating."

"But it's a perfect day for cooking out."

"Any day that Dorothy and Toto aren't blowing past our kitchen window is a perfect day for cooking out as far as you're concerned. Don't try to kid me. You just want to eat out so you don't have to clean up the kitchen afterwards."

"Oh, all right, just forget about it," she says. "We'll eat inside. I'm sure that somewhere in the back of the refrigerator there's some of that macaroni and sardine casserole I made last month. All I have to do is scrape the green stuff off the top and put it in the . . ."

Before she can finish, I have located the grill in the garage and carried it to the backyard.

The grill is one of those little portable numbers, with detachable tripod legs that fold up and make it easier to carry. When we bought it, it came with two pages of assembly instructions. With which I started the fire the first time we used it.

Working from memory, I try to attach the tripod to the grill. Each time I get two of the legs into their proper slots, the third one slips out. After forty-five minutes of trying to figure it out, I conclude that what I have here is a Rubik's grill. I settle for having two of the legs in their proper slots and the third in the general vicinity.

I set the grill on top of the picnic table, pour in three pounds of charcoal, splash on half a gallon of charcoal lighter, pile on the Sunday *New York Times*, and drop in a match. The blast is loud enough to put the Russians on red alert. With a fire going in the grill that would have warmed the cockles of Mrs. O'Leary's cow, I go inside and tell her that I am ready to prepare the meat. She hands me half a pound of hamburger.

"What's this?" I ask.

"It's the meat," she says. "I figure they'll eat two patties each."

"Are you kidding? There are five of us. If I have to make ten patties out of this, we're going to wind up with see-through hamburgers. How do you expect them to get filled up?"

"We'll give them lots of ketchup."

I press the meat into ten patties and place them in a stack separated by wax paper. While I am searching through the refrigerator for the ketchup, the eleven-year-old wanders into the kitchen and spots the meat on the table.

"What's that?" he asks.

"Hamburgers, separated by wax paper."

"Which is which?"

"The wax paper is the stuff that isn't turning brown around the edges."

"Does this mean we're cooking out today?"

"As a matter of fact, we are."

"On the grill?"

"No, I thought we'd set fire to the garage."

"You don't have to get all grumpy about it. The only reason I even mentioned it is because I thought you might like to know that your grill fell over."

I drop the ketchup and race to the backyard. The third leg of the tripod has collapsed, the grill has tipped over, and three pounds of charcoal is sitting in the middle of the picnic table, sending up enough smoke to communicate with every Indian tribe east of the Mississippi.

Fortunately, the garden hose is attached to the faucet at the end of the patio. Unfortunately, the eight-year-old has been using it to practice Cub Scout knots. The only other source of water in sight is the birdbath. I shoo away two robins, drag the birdbath to the patio, and pour the water on the picnic table.

At this point, I have a stack of hamburgers petrifying in the kitchen, a picnic table with a hole in the middle, a yardful of dirty birds and a patio full of kids who say they are so hungry they'd be willing to be adopted. By a family in Biafra.

I prop the grill back up, load it with some more charcoal, pour on enough lighter fluid to ignite Australia, and drop in another match. Forty-five minutes later the last fire truck has left and the charcoal is starting to turn white around the edges.

I put a hamburger on the grill. Instantly, half the meat sags through the wire slots and falls into the charcoal. There is a puff of smoke and a burst of flame. The flame disappears. Along with the rest of the hamburger.

"I don't think these hamburgers are going to turn out too well," the eleven-year-old says.

"Yeah," agrees the sixteen-year-old. "But the charcoal should taste pretty good."

Half an hour later we sit down to a meal of pickle spears,

potato chips into which the eight-year-old has spilled his orange drink, and the eight surviving hamburgers. The first four off the grill are slightly underdone and taste like they were cooked over a butane lighter. The other four are black on the outside, black on the inside, and shatter when you bite them.

You just can't beat a carefree meal cooked outside on the patio.

No matter how bad it is, though, cooking out is better than dining out.

Not that our family dines out often. Not when the check for our family amounts to figures that only David Stockman would recognize. Not only that, my kids don't seem all that interested in going to a restaurant where you have to get out of your car to place your order. Having grown up in an era where the first family of the stage is the Jeffersons and the music that will live forever is written by Elton John, their idea of dining out is somewhat different from mine. To them, a fancy restaurant is one that has a sign on the door that says: "No shoes, no shirt, no service." Their two favorite gourmets are Burger Chef and Jeff.

I, on the other hand, feel it's important for a kid to know what it's like inside a restaurant where the food and the container do not taste the same. I think it's good for them to know that there is food that can be eaten without taco sauce.

So one day we put as many of them as we can catch in the station wagon and drive to a nice Italian restaurant I think they might enjoy.

At the restaurant, the hostess seats us and introduces us to our waitress, who takes our drink orders.

"Hey, Dad," the eight-year-old asks after she has walked away, "who was that lady?"

"She's our waitress. She's going to bring us our food when it's ready."

"You mean they don't call out your number on the loud-speaker when it's ready?"

"Nope. She brings it right to your table."

"Weird."

"Well, it's something new they're working on. If it catches on here, they might try it at other restaurants."

Our conversation is interrupted by the eleven-year-old, who informs us that if he doesn't get something to eat right away, he will pass out from hunger.

"Eat some crackers," I suggest.

We study our menus. There is a veritable cornucopia of Italian delights, everything from linguini vongole to rigatoni alla Romano.

"I hear the saltimbocca is very good here," I tell the sixteen-year-old. "Or, how about the veal scallopini?"

"What's that junk?"

"It's not junk. Those happen to be terrific Italian specialties."

"I'm not eating any foreign food."

"Well, what do you want, then?"

"Ravioli."

Our conversation is interrupted by the eleven-year-old, who is starting to see spots in front of his eyes because of lack of food.

"Eat some breadsticks," I suggest.

The eight-year-old tugs at my sleeve.

"I hafta go to the bathroom," he says.

"OK, I'll take you."

"You don't have to. I can find it myself," he says, jumping out of his chair and running off in the general direction of the kitchen. There is no thrill compared with watching a knee-high eight-year-old dashing through a procession of waitresses carrying steaming trays of lasagna al forno.

Eventually, our waitress reappears to take our orders. I ask for linguini and white clam sauce. The sixteen-year-old asks for ravioli and Italian sausage. The eleven-year-old asks for spaghetti and meatballs. The eight-year-old asks for lasagna and Jell-O. The woman who promised to love, honor, and pick up my check asks for a double vodka and a separate table.

While we wait for the food, the eleven-year-old informs us that if he doesn't have nourishment soon, he is going to have an out-of-body experience.

"Eat some antipasto," I suggest.

The food arrives. We eat our food with gusto. Except for the eleven-year-old, who spends twenty-five minutes in combat with one spaghetto.

"Don't you like your spaghetti?" I ask.

"I'm not hungry. I think I ate too much bread."

We finish dinner, have a cup of coffee, and leave. Halfway home our conversation is interrupted by a plaintive voice from the backseat. It is the eleven-year-old.

"Dad? Can we stop at Taco Bell pretty quick? I'm starving."

But even if you have kids who do appreciate the finer points of dining, there are times you have a need for a nice, quiet meal away from them. No matter how much you love your children, every so often you have a day when you don't want to sit at a table with anybody too young to remember Debbie Reynolds.

I realize we have reached that point on the night when I see the woman who promised to love, honor, and warm my Geritol setting the table for dinner: five plates, five glasses, five sets of silverware, and two sets of ear plugs.

"What's with the ear plugs," I ask. "You expecting the macaroni and cheese to explode?"

"I don't know about you, but I need them," she says. "I don't think I can stand to listen to another meal this week. The sound of those kids slurping almost drove me up the wall last night."

"I think you're overreacting. Even some adults slurp their soup."

"They were slurping their meat loaf."

"I'll call a babysitter."

We leave the kids with the sitter and drive to a restaurant with soft lights, hanging plants, and nothing on the menu that resembles a Big Mac. After a quiet drink at the bar, a hostess leads us to a table overlooking an empty dance floor.

Just as I am about to signal for a waiter, a young man climbs up onto a platform on the other side of the dance floor and turns on a microphone. He is, he announces, a disc jockey and he will be playing music for our enjoyment.

"That's nice," I say to the woman who promised to love, honor, and turn my table. "A little dinner music will be relaxing."

The disc jockey puts on a record and flips a switch. A blast of music loud enough to turn my Chablis to vinegar bursts out of several hundred hidden speakers. My idea of dinner music is two violins and a harp somewhere in the background. His idea of dinner music apparently is the original soundtrack of the land-ing at Normandy.

A waiter arrives at our table.

"HOW'S THE LINGUINI?" I shout above the din.

"I'M SORRY, SIR, JEANNIE'S NOT HERE TONIGHT."

With the hand I am not using to keep my water glass from vibrating off the table, I point to the place on the menu that lists the linguini. The waiter nods his head and walks away.

The disc jockey puts on another record. It's some guy shouting about how, if his baby don't come back to him no more, he's gonna quit his job, kill his dog, slash his wrists, and let the blood run right down to the floor. It sort of makes me wish I hadn't ordered my linguini with red sauce.

The waiter returns with our food.

"WOULD YOU BRING US ANOTHER BOTTLE OF WINE?" I scream.

"YES, I DO," he yells. "IT'S 10:15."

Olivia Newton-John comes on the speaker system next, urging me to get physical. Which strikes me as being fairly ironic, seeing that at this very moment my salad plate is doing a 100-meter sprint toward the edge of the table, my stomach is doing jumping jacks, and my right bicep is pumping up from eating linguini in four-four time. We finish our meals in world record time, and I motion for the waiter.

"WE'RE READY FOR THE BILL," I bellow.

"BILL'S NOT HERE TONIGHT, EITHER. I THINK HE WENT OUT WITH JEANNIE."

Finally, we get the bill, pay it, and leave the restaurant with our stomachs full of nervous linguini and our ears full of ringing.

"I don't know where Jeannie and Bill went tonight," I say to the woman who promised to love, honor, and tune my hearing aid, "but I'll bet they had a better time than we did."

"Eleven o'clock," she answers.

# 12

## I THINK I'M FLUNKING SIXTH GRADE

I guess the biggest problem I have relating to Robert Young's style of fatherhood is that I don't remember ever seeing him actually *doing* anything with his kids.

I mean, the guy sat around all day in his cardigan sweater acting wise and solving problems and smiling paternally when Kitten came home with the first B in the history of Anderson family report cards. But did he ever take Princess Betty to a rock concert where the music was played loud enough to cause tooth decay? Did he ever go to a Little League game and watch Bud's team lose a no-hitter—38-37? How many times did he take Kitten roller skating at a rink where 250 junior high kids are determined to break the land speed record.

I'll bet he never even went with them to an elementary school open house.

I sat down and figured it out one day. So far there have been roughly 7,935 days in my paternityhood. Of which slightly more than half have been spent attending open houses. I have read 10,000 essays on blue-lined paper entitled "My

Scariest Halloween." I have looked at enough leaves made of orange crayon and green construction paper to carpet Sherwood Forest. I have squeezed my legs under so many elementary school desks that there are permanent callouses on the tops of my knees.

And the worst part is that they always manage to schedule them on days when I have not been called out of town on business.

"I don't see why we have to go to every one of them," I protest to the women who promised to love, honor, and clap my erasers. "They're always the same. We look at the kids' artwork, we read their essays, and we meet their teacher, who tells us what a pleasure it is to have our kids in her class. Then we stand in line for an hour and a half in the gym for a glass of warm punch and two chocolate chip cookies with fingerprints on them. Why don't we skip the next one?"

"Maybe you're right," she agrees. "Of course, by not going we are giving them the unspoken message that we have no interest in their activities, which quite possibly will serve to aggravate whatever feelings of insecurity they may already harbor as a result of the fact that you were the only father in the neighborhood who did not go with them this summer on the Father–Son 500–mile backpacking trip. But maybe they won't manifest themselves until later in life, when they have difficulty interacting with their peers and begin to display their latent hostile tendencies in sociologically unacceptable behavior. It seems to me I read somewhere that Yasser Arafat's father never went to his open houses."

Living with her has been a real pain since she started subscribing to *Psychology Today*.

So when the next open house comes around, we are there. When we arrive, the halls are crammed with kids and parents. Big kids and little kids. Old parents and new parents. You can always tell the new parents. They're the ones who come to open houses wearing dresses and high heels or suits and ties. Old parents know better. Old parents wear construction boots and shin guards. They know that moving through the halls on open house night is like swimming up Niagara Falls. No matter what room you're going to, everyone else is coming from it. Fifty percent of them are parents who don't see you coming and step on your feet. The other 50 percent are kids who do see you coming and step on your feet.

We fight our way upstream to the eight-year-old's room first. We read his essay. We look at his leaves. We take turns squeezing behind his desk. We peel gum off of our slacks. We stand in line to meet his teacher. When we are face-to-face with his teacher, we see that there is a smile on her lips. Her eyes are sparkling. It is obvious that she is thrilled to death to be here tonight for open house. Either that or her ship just came in from Colombia.

"It's very nice to meet you," she says. "Your child is a pleasure to have in the classroom."

Teachers at open houses never tell the truth. If your kid has torched the school that afternoon, a teacher will stand in the smoldering embers at open house and tell you that your child is a pleasure to have in the classroom. Or, at least, he used to be when there was a classroom.

We thank the eight-year-old's teacher and struggle against the current to the eleven-year-old's classroom. We read his essays, look at his leaves, and sit at his desk. Then we meet his teacher. She is another graduate of the Nancy Reagan School of Facial Expressions.

"My son tells me you are an avowed Communist and devil worshipper who starts class each day by strangling a live gerbil with your bare hands and forcing each of your students to stick their fingers into the electric pencil sharpener," I say.

"It's very nice to meet you," she says. "Your child is a pleasure to have in the classroom."

I guess I'm not the only one who has been to too many open houses.

Of course, there's more to school than open houses when you're a father. There's also homework.

For some reason, when I finished school I just sort of assumed that I had seen the last of homework assignments. Four kids later, I realize that it was only the beginning. If I had done as much homework then as I am doing now, I probably could have finished geometry in less than two years.

But, no matter how much I try to avoid it, homework keeps coming home. Like on the evening the eleven-year-old comes into the living room and asks me what a lobster eats. Instantly, I realize that there can only be two possible reasons for his question. Either a lobster has followed him home from school and he wants to keep it as a pet, or he needs help with a homework assignment.

"Why do you want to know?" I ask.

"I've got to write this school report about ocean life."

"Well, to tell the truth, the only thing I know about lobsters is that they live in melted butter and I can't afford them. Have you tried looking up the information?"

"I couldn't find anything," he says. Which means that there were no articles about lobsters in this week's *TV Guide*.

"Why don't you try the encyclopedia set?" I suggest. "The one that the salesman assured me was going to turn all of my children into Rhodes scholars. The one that hasn't been used since your brother needed something to stand on to reach the . . ."

"Why won't you help your son do his homework?" interrupts a familiar voice from the kitchen. It is the woman who promised to love, honor, and hang my book reviews on the refrigerator door.

"It's not that I don't want to help him," I explain. "It's just that I think he'll get more out of it if he looks it up by himself. Besides, I never was very good in science."

"I don't believe you," she says. "You're just trying to get out of helping him."

"Honest. The only reason I passed chemistry is because I sat behind a round-shouldered honor student."

"I don't believe you," she says.

"I'm not kidding. I was the only kid in class who fell asleep during sex education."

"I believe you," she says. "But if you don't help him, he's going to get the impression that you consider homework to be a waste of time and not every bit as important as the work he does in class. That's why teachers assign homework, you know."

"Really? I thought it was just to get even with parents who didn't vote for the school levy."

After dinner the eleven-year-old and I sit down to work on his report about ocean life. Which actually proves to be more interesting than I expected. By eight o'clock I learn so much about the mating habits of lobsters that I never will be able to look another Surf 'n Turf in the eye again. By 8:30 I know enough about plankton, diatoms, and bathyscaphes to give lessons to Jacques Cousteau. By nine o'clock I discover that I am all alone in the living room.

"Where's the eleven-year-old?" I ask the woman who promised to love, honor, and take attendance.

"He had to go to bed. I told him you'd be happy to finish his report for him."

Two hours later, the report is finished, I slip it into his school bag, and go to bed. When he comes home from school the next day, I meet him at the door.

"So, how did we do on our science report?" I ask him.

"Well, we had to read the reports out loud, and I got a B on presentation," he says.

"That's great."

"But I got a D on material."

Not only am I the only father in danger of flunking sixth grade, I also may be the first one ever to be drummed out of Cub Scouts.

Having grown up in a neighborhood where the only kids wearing uniforms had just escaped from somewhere, I knew next to nothing about Cub Scouts before I became a father. I had only vague impressions. A walk in the woods. An evening around a campfire. A night with your dad in a pup tent. Nobody ever said anything about Cub Scout projects.

The first I hear of them is on the day our first Cub Scout comes home from a den meeting with a little paper bag containing a block of wood, four plastic wheels, and some decals.

"What's this and how did you break it?" I ask when he dumps it on the table in front of me.

"I didn't break it," he says. "It's a Pinewood Derby kit, and we're supposed to put it together and race it next week at the pack meeting."

Each year he brings home a little paper bag, and each year we make a Pinewood Derby racer to take to the pack meeting, and each year our model is selected as the car most likely to blow up if struck from the rear. Eventually, he tires of having the only car in the Pinewood Derby that comes to a full stop halfway down a track that is inclined at a forty-five-degree angle. He retires from Scouting at the age of eleven.

His uniform, unfortunately, is taken by his younger brother. This time, however, I am the one who is prepared. I point out to our second Scout that I will be happy to walk with him on wooded trails in mud up to my lanyard. I will be thrilled to sit on a hard stump around a campfire and fill my lungs with the smell of old burning logs. I will be overjoyed to share a pup tent with him and half the mosquitos in the free world.

But under no circumstances will I help him build a Pinewood Derby car.

He agrees to these terms and joins Cub Scouts. Two pack meetings later he comes home with a little brown bag.

"That better not be a Pinewood Derby kit," I warn.

"Don't worry, it's not," he says.

"That's good."

"It's a Sailboat Regatta kit." He dumps the contents of the bag—a block of wood with a hole in the middle and a round stick—on the table in front of me.

"There's nothing to it," he says. "All we have to do is put it together and paint it."

"I guess that sounds simple enough," I agree. "Let's get it over with."

We sit down to work on his boat. It takes us exactly one hour: two minutes to put the stick into the hole, eight minutes to spray paint it blue, and fifty minutes to clean spray paint off the refrigerator, the cupboards, the kitchen floor, and the back of a dog who is not as alert as she used to be.

"It looks pretty good," I admit when we have finished.

"Yeah," he agrees. "Now all we have to do is put on the sail."

"Right. Where is it?"

"Where is what?"

"The sail we're supposed to put on it."

"That doesn't come with the kit," he says. "You have to make it out of whatever you happen to have around the house. The den leader said to use your imagination."

I use my imagination. I imagine the den leader with a little blue sailboat sticking in his ear. My Scout, meanwhile, scrounges through the house in search of sail material.

For the first hour, my Scout sits across the table from me and watches with eager anticipation as I attempt to make a sail out of two plastic sandwich bags and a paper clip.

For the second hour, my Scout sits across the table from me and watches with stoic patience as I attempt to make a sail out of twelve inches of aluminum foil and a yard of dental floss. Both used.

For the third hour, my Scout sits across the table from me and watches with thinly veiled contempt as I attempt to make a sail out of two rolls of waxed paper and three Popsicle sticks.

By the fourth hour, my Scout is in bed, leaving me at the table all alone to fight it out with a pair of worn pajama bottoms and a yard and a half of curtain-rod cord.

It is shortly after midnight before I have finished. I have spent six hours making a boat that undoubtedly will sink faster than the *Titanic*.

Some day, I console myself, I will look back on all of this

and realize that some of the happiest hours of my fatherhood were spent helping my sons with Scout projects. Actually, some day I will look back and realize that *most* of the hours of my fatherhood were spent helping my sons with Scout projects.

Almost as tough to handle as Cub Scout projects are Cub Scout meetings. Because with every Cub Scout meeting there is a frozen pizza.

Whenever I come home from work to a hearty dinner of frozen pizza and applesauce on paper plates, it can mean one of only two things: (1) There is a worldwide shortage of macaroni and cheese or (2) this is going to be a quick dinner because at seven o'clock we have to be at a parent-teacher conference, open house, choir concert, gymnastics meet, football game, or the monthly meeting of the Planned Parenthood Dropouts Club.

So when I see pizza thawing on the sinkboard one cold November day, I ask hopefully, "Arabs corner the market on macaroni and cheese?"

"Nope," says the woman who promised to love, honor, and tickle my palate. "We're having a quick dinner tonight because at seven o'clock we have to be at the Cub Scout pack meeting."

"I'd just as soon skip it," I say. "I've been slaving all day over a hot typewriter, and all I want to do after dinner is sit down and watch television and wait for the stomach pains to go away."

"But this is the night he's getting his Bobcat badge," she says. "Do you have any idea how crushed he'll be if you're not there for that? There's no telling what kind of emotional damage it might do to him. Instead of growing up into a strong, honest, well-adjusted young man, he's liable to turn into one of those wild kids you're always reading about, running around drinking and staying out till all hours."

"Well, at least it will give us something we can do together," I say.

"Very funny. But you'll be whistling a different tune when he turns out to be like my Cousin Arnold. Uncle Elmer would never go to his Cub Scout meetings with him and . . ."

"I know, I know, Cousin Arnold turned out to be a PLO terrorist."

"Not at all. My Cousin Arnold has never done a mean thing in his life. Every day he comes home from work and has dinner with Uncle Elmer and Aunt Trudy, and then they all sit around and play Parcheesi until bedtime."

"How old did you say your Cousin Arnold is?"

"Thirty-three."

"I'll warm up the car."

Following our dinner of frozen pizza, topped with cheese, pepperoni, and calcium sulfate, we drive to the Cub Scout meeting, which is held in the elementary school gym. Most of the other Scouts and their parents already are there when we arrive. It is easy to tell the Scouts from the parents. The Scouts are wearing blue uniforms and yellow scarves. The parents are wearing desperate looks and ear plugs. Not that these are necessarily the loudest Scouts in the world, but everytime they hold a meeting, the rock bank that lives next door to the school calls the cops to complain about the noise.

Like most Cub Scout pack meetings, this one has a theme. In honor of the impending elections, the meeting has taken on the air of a mock political convention. There are signs and banners, posters and slogans. After a mock debate, each Scout is given a sign to wave. It is time for the mock spontaneous demonstration.

"All right, boys," announces one of the Scout leaders, "here's your chance to make all the noise you want."

An immediate hush falls over the gym. Fifty Scouts who haven't shut up for the past three years suddenly are rendered speechless.

"Go ahead, boys, let's hear it," the Scout leader urges.

The boys continue their deathly silence, fifty Marcel Marceaus unable to summon up a whisper among them. The mock political convention ends. It is time to give out the awards. This is the reason we have come. As soon as our Scout receives his Bobcat award we can smile at him proudly, pat him on the head, tell him how pleased we are, and then get the heck out of here.

The awards are to be given out by dens. There are eight dens. We are in den number seven.

The first Scout is called up. He receives a Bobcat badge. The next Scout receives not only a Bobcat badge but a Sportsman badge and an Outdoorsman badge. The Scout after him receives a Bobcat badge, Sportsman badge, Outdoorsman badge, the Croix de Guerre, the Congressional Medal of Honor, and a Fulbright Fellowship. By the time they get to Den Six, they have given out every award this side of the Nobel Peace Prize. Helping the time fly by is the fact that the temperature in the gym is up to 180 degrees, the place reeks of used bubble gum, and my pants have fused to my folding metal chair.

"Only a few more kids to go until they get to our den," I whisper to the woman who promised to love, honor, and do her best to do her duty.

"Oh, didn't you hear?" she says. "Our den leader didn't have a chance to get all the awards turned in. Ours won't be getting their Bobcat badges until next month's meetings."

I can survive another pack meeting, I guess. But I'm not sure how many more frozen pizzas I can take.

Even if it wasn't for Scouting, there would be lots of fatherhood things I wouldn't be able to handle. I am nothing if not versatile. Some of them, like kite-flying, I have been unable to do all my life.

Even when I was a kid, I was a lousy kite-flyer. All the other kids in the neighborhood would put together a kite in two minutes, then take it out and fly it for hours, or until it got stuck in the top of a tree. I would put my kite together for two hours, then take it out and fly it for two minutes, or until it got stuck on the top of a fire hydrant.

None of which really bothered me all that much. Not until I became a father and on the first windy day of every spring at least one of my kids would come to me with faith in his eyes and hope in his heart and ask me to help him fly his kite.

Most recently it is the eight-year-old. I try to explain to him that it would be better for his personal growth and maturation if he flew the kite by himself, thereby feeling the sense of accomplishment so necessary to his continued development.

"Jeff's daddy helps him fly his kite," the eight-year-old points out.

Jeff's daddy is one of those parents who rides bikes with his kids, volunteers to go on father-son campouts in February, and jumps to his feet to lead the applause when the elementary school orchestra has just finished murdering "We Three Kings of Orient Are." Some day they will find Jeff's daddy in a dark alley, beaten to a pulp. By a bunch of guys who have no desire to go on a father-son campout until the kid is old enough to buy his own beer.

Against my better judgment, I take the eight-year-old to a kite store.

"Help you?" the salesman asks.

"We'd like a kite."

"Certainly, sir. Here's a very nice parafoil for only $37.59."

"I want a kite, not a DC-10."

"Maybe if you gave me an idea of what kind of kite you're looking for. We have dragon kites, butterfly kites, octopus kites . . ."

"I want a kite kite. One of those things that's shaped like the markings on a seven of diamonds and gets tangled in telephone wires. Like the kind you see in Norman Rockwell paintings."

The salesman stiffens and looks at me as if I had just walked into Maxim's of Paris and ordered two burrito supremes to go.

"We don't carry that kind of thing," he says. "Perhaps if you tried one of those cheap discount stores."

We go to a cheap discount store, where we are able to find a kite for a mere $2.98. We take it home. Two hours, three rolls of Scotch tape, and a gallon of Elmer's glue later, the kite is assembled. Not only do I have my doubts that I will be able to fly this kite, I'm not even sure I'll be able to lift it.

We drag the kite outside.

"OK," I tell the eight-year-old. "You hold this end of the string and Dad will run with the kite to get it up in the air."

I find an open area where there are no trees, telephone wires, or fire hydrants and begin to run into the wind with the kite string sliding slowly through my fingers. Like a 747, it lifts ponderously into the air. Like a Concorde, it levels off. Like a World War II Japanese kamikaze plane, it noses over and dive bombs into a bed of innocent tulips.

"Freak downdraft," I assure the eight-year-old.

I try it again. This time the kite climbs to waist height then flops back to earth and bounces across the grass like a stone skipping over water.

Forty-five minutes later, I have run far enough to qualify for the Boston Marathon, the kite has done more bouncing than the cast of "Three's Company", and the eight-year-old has deserted his end of the string and gone into the house. I find him in the kitchen, talking on the telephone. To Jeff's daddy.

If there's one thing I figured I would be able to do as well as Jeff's daddy, it was take my kids to the circus. Circuses, I always thought, are what being a parent is all about.

At least, that's the way it is in the movies. Producers are forever cranking out three-ring epics with close-ups of little faces thrilling to the aerialists. Little eyes wide with wonder at the daring animal trainers. Little mouths shrieking with laughter at the antics of the clowns.

Now, I'm not trying to tell Hollywood how to run its business, but I have been taking kids to the circus for more than a decade. As nearly as I can tell, not one of them ever actually has seen an aerialist do a triple somersault from one trapeze to the other, watched a wild animal trainer stick his head into the mouth of a ferocious lion, or noticed a clown getting a baggy pantsfull of seltzer water.

On the other hand, they have eaten forty acres of cotton

candy, gone home with enough souvenir coloring books to fill the Library of Congress, and spent enough money on cheap plastic toys to balance the federal budget. When my kids are too old for the circus, I predict that the economy of Taiwan will collapse instantly.

But each year the circus comes to town, and each year the woman who promised to love, honor, and crack my whip convinces me that taking our kids to the circus is the only way to keep them from a life of unemployment, crime, and drug addiction. So when the circus arrives, I find myself in the second row, between the eight-year-old and the eleven-year-old.

"OK, you guys," I warn them. "This year's going to be different. This year you're going to watch every bit of the circus. Understand?"

They both nod their heads to indicate that they understand. Somehow, I am not reassured. I don't like the sound of those nods.

The circus begins with the traditional parade. Elephants and lions, clowns and acrobats pass in glittering review, smiling and waving to the crowd. I turn to the eleven-year-old.

"Isn't this great?"

"Where's the saber-tooth tigers?" he demands.

"The what?"

"The saber-tooth tigers. I thought circuses were supposed to have saber-tooth tigers in them. What a gyp. I'll bet this isn't even a real circus."

"Of course it's a real circus. Can't you see the clowns? Can't you hear the band? Can't you smell the elephants?"

"I thought that was the eight-year-old. Anyway, I saw a circus on television and it had saber-tooth tigers in it. Where are they?"

"How should I know? Maybe they got eaten backstage by the mastodons. Just watch the circus."

The parade ends. The first act comes on. It is a group of death-defying aerialists who will perform death-defying feats above the crowd. I feel a tingle of excitement as they make their entrance. I feel the anticipation build as they climb the ladders. I feel the sense of danger as they prepare for their first death–defying feat. I feel a tugging on my sleeve. It is the eight–year-old. He has to go to the bathroom.

We fight our way through the crowd, which proves to be a pretty death–defying feat in its own right. By the time we return to our seats, the aerialists are taking their final bows after their last stunt. It was, the guy behind us assures me, a pretty decent reverse quadruple somersault through a wall of flame forty feet off the ground with no net.

The wild animal trainer is next. He runs into a cage filled with ferocious lions and snarling tigers. At his command, a lion and a lioness begin nuzzling each other affectionately.

"Look at that," I say to the eleven–year-old. "See what they're doing?"

"Yeah, sucking face," he says. "Can I have some popcorn?"

I signal for the popcorn vendor. While he stands in front of us, making change, the wild animal trainer concludes his act. I don't get to see it, but the woman next to me says it was a pretty decent finale.

"What was it?" I ask. "The old head–in–the–mouth trick?"

"Right. Only this time, the lion stuck his head into the trainer's mouth."

The circus continues. While the acrobats are building a human pyramid nine persons high, we are buying soft drinks from the pop vendor. While the clowns are convulsing the audience with laughter, we are buying magic flashlights that are guaranteed to break before we make it to the parking lot. While the elephants are standing on their front legs, rolling over, and doing an Irish jig, we are buying chameleons that are guaranteed to escape from their jars the instant we get home, turn the color of the living room carpet, crawl under the couch, and not be seen again until three weeks after rigor mortis has set in.

Finally it is all over. My arms are full of plastic souvenirs, my kids are full of cotton candy, my wallet is full of empty spaces. And I am more convinced than ever that a circus is no place for kids.

Not that the circus is a total waste of time. If nothing else, watching the wild animal trainer is good preparation for Wednesdays. Wednesday is the day that the woman who promised to love, honor, and mark my calendar has decided should be her night out.

"For nineteen years I've been supervising homework, giving baths, combing hair, brushing teeth, and making sure that nobody goes to bed with striped pajama tops and plaid bottoms," she says when she makes her decision. "I'm sick of it. I need just one night away from the kids."

"I understand completely," I agree. "From now on, we'll hire a babysitter on Wednesday nights and you and I can go out together."

"You don't understand completely," she says. "I said I wanted a night away from the kids. *All* the kids. And please stop tugging at your shirt like that. You're going to stretch the neck all out of shape."

"What are you saying? You mean you want to go out without me?"

"That's exactly what I mean. I was talking with a friend of mine, and she and I decided that we're going to go out together every Wednesday evening. We'll go bowling or to a movie or maybe we'll just stop at some nice quiet place and have a drink."

That Wednesday evening after dinner she tosses the dishes into the sink and heads for the front door.

"You're really serious about this, aren't you?" I say.

"I certainly am. But, don't worry, you shouldn't have much trouble getting the kids to bed."

"Who's worried? It doesn't take that much brains to get a couple of little kids into bed."

"I'm glad to hear you say that," she says. "Don't forget to give them a bath, make sure they brush their teeth, see that they don't drink too much soda pop before they go to bed, remind the eight-year-old to put away his toys, the gin is on the second shelf, don't wait up."

She walks out the front door. It is 7:30.

At 7:35 the eleven-year-old hits the eight-year-old in the back of the head with a Nerf football, a crime that is brought to my attention by the victim.

"What happened?" I shout at the eleven-year-old. It is not that I am angry, but I have to shout to make myself heard above the screaming of the eight-year-old, who is making enough noise to drown out Ethel Merman.

"He's lying," says the eleven-year-old.

"What do you mean, he's lying? He's not even saying anything. He's just screaming."

"Yeah. But when he stops screaming, he's gonna say I hit him with a Nerf football."

"That's ridiculous. He wouldn't be making all that noise if you only hit him with a Nerf football. Those things are soft. The only way he could be hurt is if you fired it at him out of a bazooka."

"Yeah," the eleven-year-old agrees, "and I just threw it at him real easy."

I turn to the eight-year-old, whose screams have turned to sobs with intermittent snuffles. Carefully, I examine the back of his head, picking through the matted hair.

"Is it (snuffle, snuffle) blood?" he asks, his voice quavering.

"Peanut butter."

At eight o'clock I tell them to get ready for their baths. While they undress, I run the water. By the time the tub is filled with warm, bubbly water, they each have removed one shoe.

"I thought I told you guys to get undressed."

"We're going as fast as we can," the eleven-year-old says.

Twenty minutes later they are in the tub. The eight-year-old is screaming because there is soap in his eyes. The eleven-year-old is complaining because I am pouring water over his head to rinse out the shampoo. Between pours he gasps that he is unable to breathe. I would be more sympathetic if this wasn't the same eleven-year-old who spent all last summer on the bottom of the swimming pool diving for pennies.

When they are semi-clean, reasonably dry, and in their pajamas, I stand behind them in the bathroom while they brush their teeth. When they have finished, I tell them to hop into bed.

"What about our snacks?" the eleven-year-old demands.

"What?"

"We didn't have our snacks yet."

"Why didn't you mention that before you brushed your teeth?"

"I dunno."

I fix them each a bowl of cereal. The eleven-year-old quickly eats his. The eight-year-old quickly spills his on his pajama bottoms. He takes them off and throws them into the washing machine while I go to look for some dry pajama bottoms. The only ones I can find are striped. His tops are plaid. If there's a fire in the middle of the night and we all have to run outside, I'll tell the firemen that he lives next door.

When their teeth are brushed again, I send them off to bed. It is 9:30. At 9:33 the eleven-year-old is back in the living room.

"You're supposed to be in bed," I say.

"I forgot to do my homework," he says.

"How could you do that?" I ask.

"I dunno."

It is not a sparkling answer. Then again, it wasn't all that terrific a question.

At 10:30 the homework is done, the kids are in bed, the house is quiet, and I finally feel as if I am in control of things, that is, I will be, as soon as I remember which shelf she said that gin was on.

# 13

## THE ROAD NOT TAKEN

A baseball player pitches for two innings with a hangover, and they talk about his courage. A politician publicly admits he's been having an affair with his secretary, his neighbor's wife, his minister's mother, and the senior class at UCLA, and they praise him for his bravery.

But if you really want to talk about courage, that kind of stuff is strictly minor league. To get into major league, all-star courage, you have to be a parent.

Because real courage is signing away the next four years of your life to the finance company for a new car and then handing the keys that weekend to your sixteen-year-old. Who just passed his driver's test last week. On his fourth try.

Courage is staying in your lawn chair and watching while your seven-year-old, your baby, stands small and soft on the edge of the high diving board and prepares for his very first jump into the deep end.

How can you know anything about bravery unless you've

been able to keep your eyes on the register while the checkout girl rings up a week's worth of groceries for a family of six?

Real courage is grounding a seventeen-year-old daughter for two weeks. And sticking to it the next day when she gets an invitation to go to next weekend's prom from the guy she's been goofy about since fifth grade.

Real courage is having a seventeen-year-old daughter.

You don't know a thing about bravery unless you've taken a ten-year-old to a Saturday matinee and actually gone inside with him instead of just dropping him off.

Courage is telling your fifteen-year-old that you're not going to change your mind, even though he is the only kid in tenth grade who doesn't own a moped.

True grit is walking down to the basement where your seventeen-year-old is studying with her boyfriend. And not making some kind of a noise first.

You think you've got guts? When's the last time you took a family of six out for dinner at a restaurant that doesn't wrap its food in waxed paper?

Courage is letting the eleven-year-old drive the rider mower all by himself. Along the edge of your flower bed.

Exceptional valor is going to your eight-year-old's Little League game and not saying a word when his coach teaches him the wrong way to hold the bat.

Courage is going out for the evening and counting on the fifteen-year-old to remember to close the upstairs windows if it starts to rain.

Courage is giving your eighteen-year-old daughter permission to go to New York City all by herself. With your credit cards.

Courage is bringing a child into the world, feeding him, clothing him, caring for him and worrying about him, disciplining him and educating him, preparing him to the best of your ability for the life ahead of him.

And then letting him live it.

What could a politician or a baseball player ever face that

takes more courage than that? What test could possibly confront them that could be tougher than watching their first child leave home?

I guess I always knew that would happen to us some day. But, for some reason, I always thought that she would leave us slowly.

She would go off to college, sure. But she would come home for Thanksgiving. And on Christmas she would show up with a carload of girlfriends from her dorm, and they would fill our house with loud music and giggles and fraternity men. And she would be there all through summer vacation, of course, drifting in and out of our lives each day, but spending every night in her own room, the one with the frilly canopy over the white bed that she has had ever since she was a little girl.

But she won't be coming home for Thanksgiving, and there won't be carloads of friends at Christmas or long summer vacations with her drifting in and out of our lives.

Because one day she simply moves out.

She enrolls in a local college and she finds a little house to rent for just eighty dollars a month, a place with a cozy L-shaped living room and a tiny little kitchen. A place that is not so far that she can't make it home whenever her laundry hamper is full. But far enough so that her parents will not be keeping track of her. Far enough to start a new life.

In just a few weeks, our lives change an awful lot. The grocery bill is just a little bit lower, and mealtimes are just a little quieter, and there aren't half as many cars leaking oil in our driveway as there used to be. When you turn on the radio in the family room, a blast of rock music does not assault you. The phone doesn't ring nearly as often. We don't wait up at night anymore.

One day we go to see the little house, her mother and I. She shows us where the day-bed will be as soon as she can afford one, and she leads us into her kitchen, one at a time. There are dishes on her shelves, bright new dishes I have never seen before. And pans that used to gather dust in the back of our cupboard.

When we have seen all there is to see and we have talked for a while, she walks us to the door and thanks us for coming and says she hopes we'll come back to visit her again when she has her house fixed up a little more.

It is quiet for a while, driving home, until finally her mother asks, "Do you want to talk?"

"I don't know. I was just thinking that, well, don't you think she's awfully young to be living in a house alone?"

"She's eighteen," her mother says. "I was only a year older than that when we got married."

"Yeah, but, look at that place she's living in. It's so small. And so old."

"It's nicer than the first place we lived in," her mother says.

"I just don't like the idea, that's all."

"She's not your little girl anymore," her mother says softly.

That night I go to her room and I take apart her bed, the one with the frilly canopy over it, and I store it away in a closet. Maybe some day, when she has a bigger place, she'll need that bed again. But not here. Not in this room. She won't be living here anymore. She has her own place now. She has her own life to live.

That is, I know, the way it is supposed to be, the way it has to be. But that doesn't mean I don't have to miss her. That I can just forget about all the times she needed me.

She needed me most when she was little.

She needed me to put her over my shoulder and to pat her gently on the back and to pace back and forth with her in the small hours of the morning so that her mother, who had paced with her all day, could get some rest.

She needed me to push the stroller over the bumpy parts and to fold it up and put it into the trunk. Along with the port-a-crib and the port-a-swing and the port-a-potty and all the rest of the two tons of gear it takes to get a twenty-pound baby from here to grandma's house.

When she took her first steps on shaky tiptoes, she needed a catcher, and I tried to always be there for the final lunge.

At Christmas she needed me more than ever. I was the one who sat up on Christmas Eve with a boxful of parts that was supposed to equal a doll buggy. And I was the one who found out that wheel "A" was supposed to be attached to axle "B" by widget "C", only widget "C" was somewhere between here and Taiwan. But it was my job to make it right, and usually I could find something on the bottom of my tool box to make it work, and by Christmas morning it was all together. And by Christmas afternoon it was broken.

At Easter she needed me to hide the eggs, and on the Fourth of July she needed me to light the sparklers, and on Halloween she needed me to hold her hand in the darkness between porches. To carry her shopping bag when it became too heavy with candy. To carry her home when her legs became too heavy.

As she grew, she still needed me a lot.

When she learned to ride a two-wheeler, I was the one who was fast enough to run along beside her with my hand on the seat. When she learned how to swim, I was the one who was tall enough to stand in the five feet of water with my hand under her chest. When she learned how to read, her mother was the one who had the patience to sit quietly with her on the couch. But I was the one who wound up with her on the floor when she wanted a horsey-back ride.

Soon she was too old for all of that. But not too old to need me.

She needed me to drive her to gymnastics practice. To cheerleading practice. To piano practice. When she lighted her candle at the Bluebird ceremony, I held the match. When she won baseball tickets for good grades, I sat with her way up in the red seats and explained why the right fielder threw it to second base instead of to the center fielder.

When she became a teenager, she didn't need me nearly as much. But, every once in a while, I had my uses.

She needed me to pick her up from pajama parties, and she needed me to take her to roller rinks, and she needed me to shuttle her from football games to pizza places, and eventually it became clear to both of us that if only I had a uniform and a little cap, I would be an ideal father.

At fifteen she needed me to buy a phone for her room, and at sixteen she needed me to teach her how to drive a stick shift, and at seventeen she needed money for tuition.

Now she is eighteen, going on nineteen, a college woman who lives on her own in a little house with an L-shaped living room and a kitchen built for one, and for months the only times we see her are when her laundry hamper is full or her checking account is empty.

And on Christmas morning she comes home with the young man she has been dating and she goes into the kitchen with her mother and there is a moment of silence, then a lot of laughter and talking. I go to the edge of the kitchen to investigate, even though, inside, I know what I will find.

I find them hugging each other, both of them laughing and both of them talking. And on her left hand I see the ring, a lovely gold band with a diamond, a diamond that is not too small, but not too big. Just big enough to choke a father.

For an instant, for the briefest of moments, I close my eyes and try to wish away the ring while I grapple with feelings that are not supposed to be there. I feel betrayed, I guess. Maybe just a little bit jealous. What does that young man know of nights spent pacing and hours spent worrying? He wasn't the one who taught her how to ride a two-wheeler and drove her to gymnastics and lighted her Bluebird candle. Where was he when her doll buggy needed a widget?

Then she is in my arms and I am kissing her cheek and the moment is gone, and I realize that what I am feeling has been felt by all the fathers of daughters before me.

Still, it takes a little while to accept the idea that, after a lifetime of bending down to hold her hand, she really doesn't need me anymore. It takes a while to accept the notion that we are running out of kids.

There was a time when we thought we had a lifetime supply. At least. We were convinced that we were destined to spend the rest of our days with babies over our shoulders and talcum powder on our sleeves. We could smell nothing in our future but sour milk and Desenex.

We couldn't wait for her to sit up. To crawl. To walk. We opened champagne and tossed confetti the first time she got a spoonful of strained apricots to her mouth right-side-up.

Progress was measured in things we no longer had to do for her. The first time we no longer had to comb her hair. The first pair of shoes we didn't have to tie. To the world at large, a voice sent back from the moon was cause for pride. We were thrilled to hear a toilet flush.

It seemed like forever before she was able to get herself up in the morning and off to school.

And then there came a little brother. And another. And another. And we went through it all again. From diapers to training pants to "oops." From 4 A.M. feedings to strained peas to meat that had to be cut into pieces that were nearly microscopic.

It seemed a never-ending job. We had become professional parents, apparently doomed to a career in which days off were few and overtime was the rule. There were no raises, no paid holidays, no Christmas bonuses. We couldn't even go on strike.

But then, when we were too busy installing them into their snowsuits to notice, it all began to change.

She graduated and moved off to her own place, her own car, her own phone, her own fiancé.

Her little brother became a teenager. Not only has it been a long time since we've had to comb his hair for him, it's been quite some time since neither of us was tall enough to see the top of his head.

The next brother is eleven already. He makes his own

breakfast and fixes his own bike and now he has his own bedroom, which he cleans practically every month. He's still not too big to fit on our laps, but that doesn't seem to happen as often anymore. Maybe it's my imagination, but his goodnight kisses seem to be a little briefer, his hugs a little less fierce. Before the year is over, I suspect, it will be, "Well, g'night, Dad," and he will clomp off to bed just like his big brother, leaving his tennis shoes on the living room floor behind him.

Then there will be only one little brother left, an eight-year-old with shaggy blond hair and a mouth full of gaps and only the smallest trace of baby fat.

Doing things for him doesn't seem to be nearly as much trouble as it once was. How hard is it, after all, to wash jelly off of a face that still looks up at you with eyes filled with trust? There will be, I am sure, plenty of time in my life to sit by myself and read the book that all my friends are talking about. But how many more chances will I get to sit on the couch with a little boy whose hair still is damp from the tub and read "Bugs Bunny"?

Now every goodnight kiss is a lot more special, every hug a bit more valuable. I find myself holding on to him just a little bit longer each morning before he goes off to school.

We want him to grow up, of course. It's just that it doesn't seem as urgent as it once did, when we were sure we had a lifetime supply of kids and we were convinced that we were destined to spend the rest of our lives with babies over our shoulders and talcum powder on our sleeves.

Not that it's all birthday parties and tender moments, this business of being a parent.

For every handdrawn Father's Day card remembered, there are 100 forgotten promises to take out the garbage, walk the dog, and be home by dark. For every warm goodnight kiss, there are half a dozen arguments about bedtime.

Being a parent is an endless meal of milk spilled and green beans pushed to the back of the plate. It is an eternal day of car pools and PTA meetings, of lights left on and toys left out.

Lots of times they don't understand you and usually you don't understand them. The hours are long, the benefits are uncertain, and every once in a while you can't keep yourself from wondering about the road not taken.

It would have been an easier road, you imagine. More glamorous, certainly.

There probably is an exclusive condominium at the end of that road, with windows that are not perpetually smudged and white shag carpeting that doesn't need a throw rug in the middle to cover the Kool-Aid stain and drapes that never have been climbed.

The clothes in the closet are custom-made and will not wind up on a teenager's floor. The refrigerator is so full of steak that there is no room for hot dogs, frozen pizza, or Pla-Doh. The car in the garage is a plush sedan, with stereo and air conditioning, not a tired station wagon with a rip in the upholstery and peanut butter on the steering wheel.

Sometimes you can't help but think of that road you might have taken, and frequently you wonder why in the world you didn't.

And then the door slams and a little boy with brown eyes and gaps in his mouth rushes into the kitchen and drops his gym bag in the middle of the floor and kneels down to rummage through the spelling papers with stars on them and the reminders from the teacher about the field trip that happened two weeks ago.

Finally, he finds what he is looking for. It is a book, with a green construction-paper cover he cut out with round-nosed scissors and half a dozen pages printed by him in pen, all bound together with two pieces of green yarn.

The title of the book is "ET Phone Home." Only he ran out of space, so the "m" and the "e" are sort of squeezed together at the edge of the cover.

"It's not very good," he says. "I could have done better." But, as he hands it to you, there is pride in his eyes. And ink on his cheek.

"ET is a creature from space," the book begins. "He came from Mars and got lost. And a man found M & M's and he tasted one. When ET met Elliot, he ate his toys. When his sister saw ET she yelled. ET poped his head up. ET and Elliot had a ride across the moon. When ET had to go home they waved good bye. ET went up in the dark sky. The End."

And on the last page there is a dedication.

"To Dad and Mom with Love."

I don't need Robert Young to tell me that there isn't a condominium in the world worth that much.